Kyle Lowry: The Inspiring Story of One of Basketball's All-Star Guards

An Unauthorized Biography

By: Clayton Geoffreys

Table of Contents

Foreword

When he first arrived in the NBA, Kyle Lowry had to situate himself. It took him a few years and three teams to do it, but before long, his true All-Star form emerged when he became a member of the Toronto Raptors. In 2015, he was selected to his first All-Star game. However, his impact had begun to be felt as early as the 2013-2014 season, as he led the Toronto Raptors to their first Atlantic Division title in seven years. While Lowry still has much time to continue to prove himself and to solidify the Raptors as serious title contenders year in and year out, his impact on his team has made him one of the increasingly popular point guards to follow in the league. Thank you for purchasing *Kyle Lowry: The Inspiring Story of One of Basketball's All-Star Guards*. In this unauthorized biography, we will learn Kyle Lowry's incredible life story and impact on the game of basketball. Hope you enjoy and if you do, please do not forget to leave a review!

Also, check out my website at claytongeoffreys.com to join my exclusive list where I let you know about my latest books. To thank you for your purchase, you can go to my site to download a free copy of *33 Life Lessons: Success Principles, Career Advice & Habits of Successful People*. In the book, you'll learn from some of the greatest thought leaders of different industries on what it takes to become successful and how to live a great life.

Cheers,

Clayton Geoffreys

Visit me at www.claytongeoffreys.com

Introduction

No journey to NBA stardom is ever quite the same. Some players have had the star pedigree ever since the day they were born, only to be given the status as a superstar even before getting into the NBA. LeBron James is an example of that kind of a star journey. He was figuratively given the brass ring even before he set foot on an NBA hard floor. This was rightfully so because he already had star quality even before he became a professional player.

There are also those whose potentials were already apparent, but needed maturing and sharpening. Kobe Bryant, Paul George, and Kawhi Leonard are examples. Everyone knew they had the talent, drive, and work ethic to become stars. But they needed time and honing before they achieved their potentials. After the passage of time, those players evolved to become some of the best of their era.

And some players had to work their way up from obscurity to be named as one of the elites in the league. Dirk Nowitzki came into the NBA as an unknown, but quickly rose to become one of the all-time greats. You also have Draymond Green and Manu Ginobili, who were both second-round picks, but reached the heights of championships and All-Star appearances nevertheless.

All it took was for them to get over the brand of being relatively unknown and work through that to exceed expectations.

Different stars had different roads to take for them to be part of the NBA's elite. Some had it easy, while some had it rough. Some took a lot of time, while some took none at all. It all depends on the individual players' pacing. It is not always about the destination, but more about the journey, as they say. But for all the different routes that different NBA players had to take to become stars, it is Kyle Lowry's own road to becoming elite that is most exciting and inspirational.

Kyle Lowry, a perennial All-Star point guard with the Toronto Raptors, is one of the best backcourt players in the NBA today. On an individual basis, nobody could discount what he could do on the floor. But it is his ability to lead a team that gets the most buzz. Ever since achieving the status of an All-Star, he has led the Raptors to some of the best seasons the franchise has ever seen. He even got Toronto to the deepest playoff run the team has ever had.

But if you told a basketball fan five years ago that Lowry would now be a perennial All-Star and an elite point guard, he might laugh at the prospect of Kyle leading a basketball team. After all, Lowry's skills as a player were not so apparent when he first started in the league. He was not even an eye-popping standout when he was in college. For most of his early career in the NBA, he was merely a backup point guard that barely even played in his rookie season. At best, he was serviceable as a starter.

While Lowry's status as a backup was slowly shedding away as he spent more years in the NBA, he began to have a different reputation. As a borderline starter, a lot of coaches believed he was uncoachable. He was always like that since his high school days. It would take until his ninth year in the NBA for him to reach his potential as an All-Star. It was during that season when his head coach gave him full control over the team, and it took a lot of understanding for the team to understand that it was all Lowry needed. Because of that, Lowry was allowed to flourish on his terms while his team rose along with him.

By the time he finished his 10th NBA season, Kyle Lowry was already a two-time All-Star, an All-NBA Team selection, the best player of an upstart Canadian NBA team, and the leader of arguably the best Toronto Raptors team ever assembled. He nearly took the Raptors to what could have been the franchise's first appearance in the NBA Finals. You do not always expect those results from a former backup point guard. But Lowry delivered and went on to prove to his former teams and past coaches that he was indeed a star.

It is easy for us to dismiss the fact that Kyle Lowry took nine seasons to get to the level of an elite point guard. But what cannot be dismissed is the fact that you never see a backup point guard working behind veteran guards for such a long time biding his way at a chance of someday becoming the leading man of his team. Lowry did that for the longest time possible. Now look how far he has gotten.

Chapter 1: Childhood and Early Life

Kyle Lowry was born on March 25, 1986, to parents Lonnie Lowry, Sr. and Marie Hollaway. Since Lonnie and Marie were separated, it fell on the mother to take care of her their two sons. Marie Hollaway, together with her mother, did her best to raised Kyle and his older brother on her own. She had to work two jobs and a lot of overtime just to get everything her sons needed.[ii] Her hard work rubbed off on Kyle, who would always say that he looked up to his mother for her work ethic.

Kyle grew up in one of the most dangerous parts of North Philadelphia, especially during the 80's when he was still in his formative years as a youngster. Back then, it was a common sight to see someone dying in the streets.[i] That was the life Kyle Lowry was accustomed to when he was young.

Thankfully, Kyle was guided accordingly by his mother and his grandmother even without the help of Lonnie Sr., who was never interested in looking after the welfare of his son. Luckily, Kyle's brother Lonnie, Jr. also chipped in to guide him away from the adverse influences of society especially in such a rough neighborhood.

Lonnie Sr., though always absent, played a significant role in Kyle's childhood nonetheless. One day, Lonnie Sr. promised his son that they would spend the day together and that he would treat Kyle like a father should. Kyle would wait the whole day for his father to come, but Lonnie Sr. never showed up. Since then, Kyle lost all hope in his father and learned how to trust himself more.[iii]

What also helped Kyle Lowry stay away from the bad vices, even without the aid of his father, were sports. Even at a young age, Lowry was a talented athlete in every kind of sport. His mother would rather spend money buying him sporting goods than toys. Kyle Lowry's family was historically composed of talented softball and baseball players. As such, Kyle's first sport was baseball. His mother Marie said that Kyle was excellent at the sport when he was still a young boy. Kyle would also try football after his years with baseball.[ii]

Out of all the games that Kyle Lowry tried when he was a kid, it was basketball that he truly fell in love with. Kyle grew up doing nothing but playing basketball. Even as a child, Lowry lived and breathed the sport. His daily routine was even centered around playing as much basketball as he could before and after school. That was how much Kyle loved to play basketball even as a young boy.

Lonnie Jr. would also help feed his younger brother's love for the game of basketball. The two grew especially close since they only had each other to lean on. Lonnie would take Kyle with him as much as he could whenever he would go to local courts or other basketball events within the city.[i] He taught his younger brother how to become a better basketball player. This only served to fuel the burning basketball fire within Kyle Lowry.

During winter whenever Kyle was not with his brother, he would go out with his friends just to look for an indoor basketball court that was open to them. Sometimes, the ordeal would take them almost two hours of going around town in a bus.[i] That was how much Kyle wanted to play basketball every day. That same love for the game was what took him to the next level when he got to high school.

Kyle Lowry's love for the game at his young age got Rick Clancy, a local coach in Philadelphia, involved in the developing player's life. Clancy acted like a father figure, not only to Kyle, but to the rest of the Philadelphia basketball youth as well. He would even trade in his family car for a van just so that he could drive the kids to and from games.

Kyle Lowry, whenever Clancy was driving, would use the time wisely. He would ask Clancy tons of questions about the ins and outs of basketball. Clancy himself was not annoyed. He was so impressed by Lowry's level of questioning and thinking that he believed that it was the young boy's level of basketball IQ and capacity to learn that set him apart from all of the other kids of his age.[i] Lowry's aptitude for the game was becoming apparent even as a young boy.

Chapter 2: High School Career

Kyle Lowry's high school career started at Northeast High School, an open and public system located in Philadelphia. Back in his early years as a high school player, Kyle Lowry did not start out as a star, much like how it took him some time before becoming an established starter in the NBA.

It would take Kyle Lowry until his sophomore year in high school for him to start blossoming into a rare talent of a basketball player. Lowry had just hit a growth spurt that season. The 5'11" point guard was beginning to grow into his body and his potential as a high school talent.

Even at that stage of his high school career, Kyle Lowry was already attracting the attention of many college scouts looking to recruit him into their programs by the time Kyle was ready to go to the collegiate rankings. As Rick Clancy would say, the recruiters were all lining up like vultures on a dead animal carcass.[i] They were ready to offer everything they could to a budding Kyle Lowry.

Though Kyle Lowry had been rising the ranks of Philadelphia's best young players, he did not let the hype and popularity get to him. Lowry focused on making himself a better player from an individual standpoint. But as Kyle was developing, negative remarks about his personality began to surface as well.

The initial thought about Kyle Lowry was that as good a player as he was, he was uncoachable. People started to say that coaches were never able to reach Lowry. He would not listen to any instructions given to him. He would always try to do things his way on the court instead of listening to what his coaches wanted him to do. That was why, for his immense talents as a basketball player, he was not the best high school prospect out there.

Kyle Lowry would later transfer to Cardinal Dougherty High School, a Catholic school whose high school basketball team played in the Philadelphia Catholic League. Even after making the transfer from the open public system to the private leagues, Kyle Lowry's star did not fall.

In his junior year, Kyle Lowry would continue to dominate Philadelphia's high school basketball scene. Though he was barely 6-feet tall, Lowry became a household name in Philly's Catholic League. That league, though full of smaller players, was a bruising one. The players and other teams did not care how big you were. They would play you physically no matter what your size as a player was. That style suited Kyle better.[iii]

He was never the tallest nor the most athletic point guard. What Kyle lacked in height and athleticism, he made up for in his physical and bruising play. He was a stocky point guard that relied more on bullying his way through to the basket. Kyle rose up to become the league's Most Valuable Player as well as the leader of the league's best high school team. It was during the final moments of the state tournament that Lowry's star quality came to fruition.

Down by 13 points when the game was in the final minutes of the third quarter in the Catholic League's Semifinal game, Kyle Lowry was suddenly whistled for his fourth foul of the contest. One more foul would have disqualified him for the rest of the night. More importantly, Dougherty would have missed the services of their star player either way. Staying in the game meant that Lowry was a liability, especially with only one more foul left. But not playing Kyle the rest of the way meant that Dougherty had no chances of winning the game.

A rare sight for a player that had the reputation for being defiant, Kyle Lowry went straight to the bench thinking for sure that he was done for the night. But his coaches persuaded him to stay on the court because they knew that the star point guard was their only hope of making it to the finals.

Kyle Lowry was suddenly given his marching orders: he was tasked to get the team back in the game. There were no special requests or strategies used. His coaches just gave him the reigns to do whatever he wanted to do. That was the type of player that Lowry was. Dave Distel, one of his closest coaches at Dougherty, said that Kyle was always an introvert that did not have a lot of friends. It was not because he was uncoachable or that he was not friendly. He was just simply the kind of guy that wanted to be left alone to do whatever he wanted.[i]

Kyle Lowry was the kind of point guard that froze and struggled whenever coaches gave him special orders. But when you put your faith in him, Lowry would go through hell and back just to show that he was indeed worthy of the coaches' trust. That was what he did in the fourth quarter of that semifinals game. Kyle Lowry was the catalyst that got Dougherty back in the match with a 25-8 fourth quarter rally. Of course, it was his three-point play in the final seconds that sealed the win for his school.[i]

There were no unusual barking orders given to Kyle Lowry in that classic fourth quarter comeback. He was not asked to do anything in particular that night. He was just given the reigns by a coaching staff that had a lot of faith in what the point guard could do. With his the trust of the team in him, Lowry delivered and gave the win to Cardinal Dougherty.[i]

Kyle Lowry's popularity and stock as a coveted high school recruit were great as ever, especially with the way he led his team to that comeback win. Despite the rise in popularity, some disgruntled schools were out to get Kyle Lowry. One big college program, which had been particularly bitter towards Lowry for the latter's refusal to join them, even started rumors that the star high school point guard was involved with illegal substances. The stories only made Kyle more and more distrusting.

Kyle Lowry, who was never the most open player, only grew to guard himself even more tightly than before. He had always been distrusting of authority, especially with how he never learned to trust his father. Lonnie Sr. always had a habit of disappointing his children despite the fact that he was only a few minutes away from Kyle and Lonnie Jr. The disappointments of hoping for a father figure had grown so much on Kyle that he never gave many people his trust. It even took Distel, who was the closest thing to a father to Lowry, years before the young point guard would fully trust him. The rumors and controversy that suddenly sprouted only served to push Kyle deeper into himself.

The bad luck did not stop there for Kyle Lowry. Though he was a prized recruit for a lot of colleges, not a lot of programs were willing to wait on him. His original plan was to go to Xavier in Cincinnati. Xavier had been actively recruiting Kyle, but his lack of commitment to the program led the school to fill out their roster spot with other recruits. It was the same story with other big names such as North Carolina, Connecticut, and Kansas. They were unsure of what Kyle Lowry could bring to the table. They would fill their roster spots long before they could even see what Lowry could offer the team.

With opportunities going away left and right, Kyle Lowry had no choice but to go to Villanova to try out for a roster spot. Originally, Lowry never wanted to play for Villanova because it was out in the suburbs. It was not the ideal place to play, especially for a kid that grew up in Northern Philadelphia. But Kyle did not have any other choice.

Lowry would try out for Villanova's program in an open gym session. The program already had competent guards such as Randy Foye and Allan Ray at that time. Jay Wright, Villanova's head coach at that point, knew about Lowry's work, but he did not believe the young guard wanted to go there because he was from Philly. A kid that grew up in Philadelphia would never want to play out in Villanova. But Lowry not only showed he belonged in Villanova. He showed he had what it took to be a part of the culture and program.

Wright and former Villanova forward Curtis Sumpter were both impressed with what Kyle Lowry brought to the table. He was not the usual playground guard that always wanted to wow people with dozens of crossover moves and highlight dribble plays. Lowry was just a hard-nosed kid that knew how to play the game in the right and physical way. He could read defenses and make the right plays whenever he needed to. Lowry did not try to break ankles with crossovers. Instead, he just seemed like that basketball came naturally for him.[iii]

Because of what Wright saw in Kyle Lowry, Villanova actively courted the young guard through their young assistant Billy Lange. With the help of Distel, Lange was able to earn the trust of the distrusting Kyle Lowry. He was able to bond with the point guard and learn a thing or two from the introverted rising star. Lange did not try to influence Lowry into going to Villanova, but he tried his best to earn the trust of the point guard learning from Distel that trust was the deciding factor in winning Kyle Lowry's favor. Because of Lange, Lowry would choose Villanova as his destination for college after averaging 19 points, eight rebounds, six assists, and five steals in his final year in high school. Cardinal Dougherty went 26-6 with the league MVP leading the way.

Chapter 3: College Career

Kyle Lowry was coming into Villanova to join a crop of great backcourt players like Randy Foye. With Lowry and Foye at the helm of Villanova's attack, the program was set to have one of the most-feared backcourt tandems in the entire nation. But that almost did not become the case, especially due to problems arising from Kyle Lowry.

Lowry almost considered transferring to another college program just as soon as he arrived in Villanova. The reason for almost making the change was that Kyle Lowry did not like it that a lot of people were telling him what to do. His "uncoachable" quality was resurfacing again. Lowry was never the type of player that performed well when told what to do by coaches. He was never comfortable with authority figures barking orders at him. He had distrusted too much authority figures to know that putting his trust in them was not an easy thing to do.

As a player, Kyle Lowry needed to be trusted and left alone to be effective. That was not the case at Villanova. He told Distel that he did not like the way coaches were always telling him to do things their way. Moreover, Lange, the only member of the coaching staff he trusted, was on his way out of Villanova to accept a coaching job at Navy. Lowry, feeling betrayed, would never talk to Lange again.[iii]

The feeling was mutual. Wright, at first, thought that Kyle Lowry was too much of a load to handle. He and his coaching staff thought that Lowry was too taxing of a player. Lowry was challenging Wright's team too much with his uncoachability. Because of that, both parties seemed to have come to a conclusion that they were better off without each other. Lowry contemplated transferring.[iii]

Distel would somehow manage to convince Kyle Lowry to give Villanova one more shot. He told the point guard that transferring to another school would take more time away from him and would probably hinder his development as a player. Because of that, Lowry would stay with Villanova despite the initial problems he faced with the coaching staff.

Kyle Lowry would brave through the year as a Villanova Wildcat. Just when he was making progress with the coaching staff, Lowry would get sidelined because of a torn ACL. While a torn ACL is always the type of injury you would want to avoid as a basketball player, it was the same injury that had Kyle Lowry warming up to his coaching staff.

Without basketball during the time of his recovery, Kyle Lowry began to believe and trust in his coaches more than ever. It was also at that time that Wright saw who Lowry truly was. Kyle was dedicated more than ever to his family during his time recovering. He did not have basketball, but he still had his family and team. His devotion to the team and coaching staff during that period made Wright realize that he had a gem in Kyle Lowry, who was not even sure if he could suit up for the team ever again.[iii]

Kyle Lowry, on his part, started warming up to his teammates and coaches. He was not the hard-headed kid that Wright initially thought he was. He saw how caring, dedicated, and hard-nosed Lowry truly was underneath the hard exterior he was trying to portray the whole time. Kyle Lowry was starting to become a part of the team, just as much as the team was becoming a part of him.

Despite the ACL injury, Kyle Lowry made a full recovery that allowed him to suit up earlier than expected. He would only miss the first parts of his rookie season and would come back to the team for an excellent freshman campaign. He was an immediate impact player for the Villanova Wildcats even as he had just recovered from the torn ACL.

Kyle Lowry made his Villanova debut on December 31, 2004. In that win over Penn State, Lowry had five points, which included an under-the-basket scoop layup for his first points in college. Lowry, throughout the season, would also prove his abilities in all facets of the game. He had four steals and six rebounds in a blowout win against West Virginia on January 5 despite scoring only six points.

As respectable a start that Kyle Lowry had that season, his fiery attitude would also get the best of him. He would be ejected in a game against Kansas for punching an opponent in the first half. He would then miss the next game as part of his automatic suspension. Nevertheless, he came back strong to score a then-season-best 12 points against Connecticut.

With Kyle Lowry playing well for a freshman that had just got back from injury, it would not be long until he would take over the starting spot after playing off the bench for most of the early part of the season. He made his first start on February 23. He scored 11 points in that win over Boston College and would not relinquish that spot since then.

Kyle Lowry's best game of the season came during the NCAA Tournament. In a match against North Carolina in the regional semifinals, Lowry delivered 18 points, seven rebounds, and three assists while displaying his ferocity as a mini pit bull on the floor. The 6-foot tall point guard would average 7.5 points, 3.2 rebounds, two assists, and 1.3 steals in a respectable rookie season with Villanova. He was selected to the Big East All-Rookie Team and was the Philadelphia Big Five Rookie of the Year.

Kyle Lowry would come back strong in his sophomore season with Villanova. After teammate Sumpter fell to a season-ending injury, Wright would make Lowry a full-time starter alongside guys like Allan Ray and Randy Foye. Lowry would become part of Villanova's dreaded four-guard starting lineup that season. With him and Foye leading the backcourt, Villanova remained one of the top programs that season.

With Lowry playing better than he ever had for Villanova that season, the school always found itself in the top 10 rankings throughout the season. At the end of the regular season, Villanova was a first seed heading into the NCAA Tournament. It was the first time that Villanova entered March Madness as the top seed, and it was all thanks to their human pit bull Kyle Lowry, who continued to play all facets of the game well that year.

Kyle Lowry would continue to lead the Villanova Wildcats to a remarkable run in the NCAA Tournament. In the first round of the tournament, Lowry played 32 minutes of hard-nosed defense while contributing 9 points and two rebounds in that win. In the second round, he would lead the Wildcats to a win over Arizona. Lowry had 8 points and four assists in that game where his efforts on defense and running a team was on full display. Unfortunately for him and Villanova, they would fall to Florida in the Elite Eight of the NCAA Tournament.

In his second season with Villanova, Kyle Lowry averaged 11 points, 4.3 rebounds, 3.7 assists, and 2.3 steals in 29 minutes of action. He was a member of the All-Big 5 First Team and a Big East Second Team selection that season. After his run as a sophomore player, Kyle Lowry would choose to forego his two years with Villanova to try his hand at the NBA Draft.

The decision to join the NBA Draft came when he realized he had garnered enough attention and accolades in two years with Villanova to have a chance to become a first-round pick. Kyle Lowry, though he still had a lot left to learn in college, believed that it was the best decision because he thought that players that stayed longer in college were under more scrutiny than those that went to the NBA as soon as possible. Wright, on his part, respected his point guard's decision, though he did not foresee Lowry leaving the program after only two seasons.

Chapter 4: Kyle Lowry's NBA Career

Getting Drafted

Kyle Lowry was set to join a 2006 NBA Draft that did not have a lot of star power compared to the previous years. Nevertheless, Lowry was up against household college names such as LaMarcus Aldridge, Adam Morrison, Brandon Roy, and JJ Redick, among others. As good as he was in college, he was not a standout compared to the other bigger names, which even included teammate and backcourt buddy Randy Foye. If anything, he was hardly mentioned among the top prospects.

Standing at 6'0" tall, Kyle Lowry was not a particularly big point guard. In fact, he was shorter than most other NBA point guards and the other playmakers of his draft class. His height was one of his disadvantages coming into the NBA Draft. Despite that, Lowry played bigger than he is. At about 190 lbs., Kyle Lowry had an NBA-ready body that he used to his advantage against smaller guards. He knows how to use his body to force his way to the basket, and he could be pretty explosive for a guy his size.[iv]

Aside from his physicality at the point guard position, Kyle Lowry was also a pretty explosive guard. In a draft class that had no other elite point guards, Lowry was probably the most explosive out of the bunch. He could get to his spots quickly and easily using his foot speed. With his quickness, he could trigger fast break situations for Villanova's dreaded four-guard lineup.[iv]

Off the dribble, Kyle Lowry can get to the basket with ease. He has enough quickness and explosiveness in his stocky body to finish strong at the rim. Even when guarded tightly, he will cross defenders over to get open scoring opportunities.

Though it was never the best facet of his game, Lowry can run an offense pretty well. He could dribble the ball flawlessly and see the floor well despite his size. He did not pass the ball at a high level, but he always seemed to make the right passes. That was why, though he did not have a lot of assists in college, his Assist/TO ratio was pretty high.[iv]

For a short point guard, Kyle Lowry could rebound at an excellent rate. He was never the tallest or the biggest playmaker, and he was never the highest leaper. But, somehow, Lowry gets the job done at the rebounding end because of his natural basketball IQ and because he knows how to use his body well to box out taller opponents.

Defense is where Kyle Lowry truly excelled. Using his quickness and his strong upper body, Lowry could keep up with even the fastest and the strongest opposing point guards in every level that he played in. He excelled as a full-court defender in Villanova's dreaded four-guard full-court defensive schemes because of his ability to pressure the ball handler, and he has hands quick enough to get more steals than any other player on the floor.[iv]

However, Kyle Lowry did still have a lot of knocks to his game. Offensively, his outside shot needed a lot of work. In Villanova, he improved his three-point shooting from 23% to 44% in two seasons. But the improvement in that facet of his game was attributable to the fewer outside shots he took in his sophomore season. He never attempted a lot of jumpers from beyond the perimeter because that was never really one of his best assets on the offensive end.

Lowry's outside shooting needed a lot of work, but so did his perimeter jumpers. Kyle Lowry almost exclusively relied on his slashing ability to get points up on the board. His off the dribble shot and his in-between game needed a lot of work. In college, you would always see defenders giving him space to shoot and daring him to beat his opponents with his jumpers.[iv] With three other guards that could shoot from the perimeter, Kyle Lowry was never compelled to improve that facet of his game. It did not hurt him in college, but the NBA game was a different animal.

Kyle Lowry seemed like a leader on paper, especially because of how well Villanova was winning with him in the lineup. But, truth be told, he was never the captain of the Wildcats in his two-year stint with the team. The leadership reigns were given mostly to Foye and Ray when Lowry was playing for the team.[iv] You would often see Kyle Lowry deferring to his other backcourt mates when things got tough.

Some may argue that it was Kyle Lowry making things easier for Foye and Raye when they were playing for two years. Others would even go and say that the presence of the other veteran guards in Villanova prevented Lowry from exploding and breaking out as a star. But the consensus was that Lowry's life was made easier because of the presence of the other top guards in the team. He could only get open shots, and he could handle getting marked by only one man because Randy Foye and Allan Ray were scoring and hitting outside shots at will. With that, Lowry never felt what it meant to be the go-to guy in college.[iv]

When he finally got a crack at the NBA, Kyle Lowry's leadership skills and ability to become the go-to guy would be sorely tested. How could he handle getting marked and defended at excellent levels when he was always the man left open in college? How could he handle the pressure of running an offense all on his own without three other guards making life easier for him? Those were the questions that had NBA teams believing that Kyle Lowry was not worth being a lottery pick.

You also add to the fray Kyle Lowry's mentality problems. Though he was always a fierce competitor on the floor, there is always a fine line between competing at a high level and knowing when to let your emotions out. When things got tough, Lowry seemed to force the issue more than he was supposed to. Those instances often led to turnovers and useless fouls. Compounding all of that was his reputation of disrespecting authority figures. Lowry was the type of player that needed time to trust and respect coaches. You do not have the luxury of time in the NBA, especially when you are asked to adjust quickly to the rigors of an 82-game season.

With all those said and done, Kyle Lowry was a good NBA prospect at the point guard position but had a lot of flaws to his game and his character. He had all the makings of what could have been a lottery pick in the 2006 NBA Draft, but all his weaknesses had coaches doubting if he was even worth consideration in the first round. All the doubts about his game had Lowry saying that the NBA Draft was the scariest thing he ever experienced in his life.[iii]

Kyle Lowry had several suitors coming into the 2006 NBA Draft. One of which were the Cleveland Cavaliers, who contemplated pairing him up with LeBron James as the superstar's complementary piece at the point guard position. But the Cavs were eventually turned off by Lowry's past health issues and his attitude towards authority.

It was debated that Kyle Lowry was the better Villanova Wildcat compared to his college teammate Randy Foye. However, Foye would end up being chosen as the seventh pick in the draft class. Meanwhile, the first round was winding down, and Lowry was not even selected within the top 20.

Nevertheless, Kyle Lowry made it to the NBA after getting chosen by the Memphis Grizzlies with the 24th pick. Surprisingly, not a lot of point guards were selected in the first round. The only pure point guard chosen ahead of Lowry was Rajon Rondo, who was the 21st pick of that draft class.

Rookie Campaign

Kyle Lowry was set to join a Memphis Grizzlies team that relied mostly on All-Star Pau Gasol for scoring, and former Rookie of the Year Mike Miller as a complement out in the perimeter. The Grizzlies did not have an established point guard to run their offense. They were relying more on veterans Damon Stoudamire and Chucky Atkins as their primary playmakers. But none of them could provide the spark and youthful injection needed by a rebuilding franchise. That was when Kyle Lowry was supposed to come in and own the top point guard spot on the team.

Even then-head Coach Mike Fratello liked and admired Lowry's style. Fratello liked Lowry's competitive edge and passion for the game of basketball. In turn, he would try his best to make Kyle Lowry understand the ins and outs of their system without acting like he was ordering him around. Lowry wanted to give back to his coach by playing his best on the hard floor. He would try to do so early in his career.[ii]

Kyle Lowry opened his professional career as an NBA player considerably well. He would play 28 minutes off the bench in a narrow loss to the New York Knicks on November 1, 2006. He delivered and did not disappoint. Lowry had 6 points, three assists, two steals, and an impressive ten rebounds for a 6'0" point guard at the end of his NBA debut.

But, despite playing well in his first game in the NBA, the Grizzlies opted to focus more of the playing time towards the tested veterans. After all, Lowry was merely a rookie that comparatively flew under the radar during his college years. Because of that, Kyle Lowry would see inconsistent minutes off the bench without making much impact as Memphis lost seven of its first eight games.

On November 20 versus the Orlando Magic, Kyle Lowry would have his then-best performance as an NBA player. In that win, he would put up 16 points, five rebounds, six assists, and five steals all in 30 minutes off the bench. He did not even force the issue that game because he merely attempted ten shots. That was but a mere glimpse of what Lowry would become after several more seasons in the NBA.

While it seemed like Kyle Lowry was on his way to becoming a promising rookie point guard, tragedy was quick to strike a hand. In his 10th game of the season against the Cleveland Cavaliers, Lowry suffered a broken wrist in only 11 minutes of play. The injury would keep him sidelined for the rest of the season. Lowry would play only ten games during his rookie season. He averaged 5.6 points, 3.1 rebounds, 3.2 assists, and 1.4 steals in his rookie campaign.

Bounce Back from Injury

During the time that he was recovering from his injury, Kyle Lowry doubted whether he had a future with the Memphis Grizzlies or not. After all, he had only played ten games out of 82 that season before bowing down to an injured wrist. He even feared that he would stagnate as a player with all the time he spent outside of the basketball court. Lowry also feared the possibility that a stint in the D-League might be looming over his future the next season.[iii]

With all those doubts and fears fueling him, Kyle Lowry would work on his individual skills as a player while still recovering from injury. Lowry was good friends with teammate Mike Miller. He spent a lot of his free time with Miller at their house. Ever the prolific outside shooter, Miller would help Lowry improve on his perimeter marksmanship. Even when he was not home, Lowry was allowed access to go to the Miller household to practice at the shooter's indoor basketball court.[iii]

Coming into his second season with the NBA and with the Memphis Grizzlies, Kyle Lowry was excited to go back to the basketball court and showcase his much-improved game. He had a good chance of becoming the Grizzlies' designated point guard, especially with the veteran point guards gone. Lowry was almost sure he was going to be the main guy manning the point that season.

Just when Kyle was ready to take over the reins of the point guard position in Memphis, the Grizzlies would select another point guard in the draft using their lottery pick. The franchise thought that Mike Conley was the best available prospect they could get without even thinking about the decision of taking another point guard just one season after drafting Lowry.[iii]

Memphis Grizzlies general manager Chris Wallace thought that Mike Conley was the best available player they could draft with their lottery pick in that year's edition of the NBA Draft. He also thought that Conley had the potential to become a star in the NBA.[iii] That was the reason why the Grizzlies put so much hope in another point guard without even realizing a stunned Kyle Lowry was in the background trying to prove his worth to the organization.

Nevertheless, Kyle Lowry did not take anything personally towards Conley. They were both just young point guards trying to make an early impact in the NBA. In fact, Lowry and Conley were good friends back then. With that, the two point guards would split the time at the playmaker's position coming into the 2007-08 season. Conley was the designated starter, but Lowry's minutes were not far behind.

In only his second game in the 2007-08 season, Kyle Lowry would display his new found skills at the offensive end. Against the Indiana Pacers in a loss on November 3, 2007, Lowry scored a then career-best 19 points on 4 out of 5 shooting from the field and in only 25 minutes off the Memphis bench. While playing the role of the first player off the bench for the Grizzlies in his first 20 games that season, Lowry would break into double digits in nine outings. In almost 50 minutes of action in an overtime win against the New Orleans Hornets on December 7, he even had a near triple-double of 14 points, nine rebounds, and nine assists against rising point guard Chris Paul.

On January 25, 2008, Kyle Lowry would have double digits in assists for the first time in his career. It was also his first double-double. Lowry had 13 points, ten assists, and 5 steals that game in a loss to Washington Wizards. After that match, Lowry would have a rare start at the point guard position. He did not disappoint. Lowry had 21 points, eight rebounds, and five assists in that overtime win over the Los Angeles Clippers. As a starter for the next five outings, Lowry would score in double digits for five straight games while showcasing what he could do as the primary point guard of the team.

Somehow, Kyle Lowry would go back to doing bench duties for the remainder of the season. But that did not stop him from turning in a new career performance on March 4. Lowry would score 24 points on 8 out of 12 shooting in only 31 minutes off the bench in a loss to the Chicago Bulls. Just a day after that, he scored 15 in a win over New Jersey.

Despite playing well even as Mike Conley's backup, Kyle Lowry would not solve the Memphis Grizzlies' problems. They were far from contending for a playoff spot despite having a few All-Star caliber players. Nevertheless, the team's young talent, which included Lowry, were what prompted them to start a rebuilding process that had them trading away their best and only reliable veteran player.

As the season was coming to an end, the Memphis Grizzlies were all but out of playoff contention, especially after trading away their star player Pau Gasol in an attempt to start over as a franchise. Because of that, Lowry played a more active role in the Grizzlies' offense. In his final 22 games of the season, Lowry scored in double digits in 15 outings despite playing bench minutes. Kyle Lowry was slowly becoming the player he is today.

After his second season in the NBA, Kyle Lowry averaged 9.6 points, three rebounds, 3.6 assists, and 1.1 steals. He found a way to coexist with Mike Conley as the two point guards played the same amount of minutes though Lowry did it all off the bench in 73 of the 82 games he played that season. In fact, some may even go on to say that Lowry was the better player after having better stats than the rookie Mike Conley. Nevertheless, Lowry was just trying his best to prove his worth as a player hoping that the organization might rethink giving the reigns to another point guard.

Final Season in Memphis, Clash with Hollins, Trade to the Houston Rockets

A rebuilding Memphis Grizzlies team had a lot of talented young pieces to work and build on coming into the 2008-09 season. First, they had a confident and developing Kyle Lowry, who was hungry to prove himself as a point guard. Then they had a Mike Conley ready to take over the reigns as the primary point guard. Above all that were their offensive pieces: rookie OJ Mayo, athletic wingman Rudy Gay, and a surprisingly impressive Marc Gasol, the brother of Pau Gasol. With such a young core, the Grizzlies were going to be a promising team in future seasons.

However, despite a strong finish to his second season in the league, Kyle Lowry was not able to replicate the same success in the first few weeks of his third year in the NBA. In his first 20 games, Lowry would score in double digits only four times while the Grizzlies were continuing to lose game after game.

Despite starting the season slowly, Kyle Lowry would remain hopeful that he could turn his career around, especially after he was given the starter's spot as the Grizzlies head coach was shuffling his lineup. Lowry did not disappoint after receiving that new role. He had a new career high of 12 assists to go along with 14 points in a loss to the Minnesota Timberwolves on December 29, 2008. On January 13, 2009, he had a then career-best 25 points in a loss to the Cavs. He hit 15 of 16 free throws that game.

Things would, however, turn for the worse for Kyle Lowry in the early part of 2009. Lionel Hollins would take over as the new head coach of the Grizzlies. This was when Lowry knew he had no future in Memphis. After all, he was a 24th pick going up against a fourth pick named Mike Conley. In fact, even Hollins himself reaffirmed the franchise's choice of establishing Conley as the leading man on the point. All this did not sit well for Lowry.[iii]

Kyle Lowry was not happy with his role on the team. He was getting fewer minutes while Conley was averaging more than 30 per game. The Grizzlies were intent on letting Lowry play in the background while he was with Memphis. Again, Kyle Lowry was uneasy about that decision. The negativity on the part of Lowry was so palpable that some people in the organization even thought that he was a bad influence for the team.[iii]

His bad reputation with the Grizzlies franchise along with his decreased role were all too much for Lowry to handle. He was merely 22 years old wanting to make a name for himself in the NBA. He was branded as a bad influence and negative presence in the franchise. Every decision that Hollins made did not sit well with him, either. He was playing with an edge on the court because his new head coach did not give him a chance to play or even talk to him on a personal level.[iii] As history tells us, Lowry was never happy when his coaches did not trust him. That was the "uncoachable" aspect to his personality.

Kyle Lowry was not contributing to the rebuilding process, either. The Memphis Grizzlies were banking on the young talent that they in preparation for their franchise's future as a contending team. However, Kyle Lowry remained a distraction. The Grizzlies were still far away from their goal of becoming perennial contenders. Lowry's negative presence in the locker room would have hindered their growth as a squad.

Because of the bad relationship between Kyle Lowry and Lionel Hollins on top of the former's unhappiness towards his role with the team, the Memphis Grizzlies decided to ship the third year point guard over to the Houston Rockets. In 49 games with the Grizzlies, Lowry averaged 7.6 points, 2.3 rebounds, 3.6 assists, and one steal. He saw his minutes dropping to about 22 a night.

General manager Wallace downplayed all of the drama. Wallace would go on to say that he believed Lowry was as deserving of a starting point guard as Conley was. The dilemma on who to develop, according to him, was causing troubles on a team that wanted to rebuild on its young pieces. And because they believed Conley was the playmaker that could steer them towards the right direction, he and the team thought that Lowry was better off elsewhere.[iii] They were right.

In Houston, Kyle Lowry had the opportunity to start fresh with a new organization, new teammates, and new coaches. He especially loved the way his new head coach Rick Adelman made it easier for him to adjust to a new environment. Adelman did not know Lowry deeply, but he tried his best to put the young point guard under his tutelage. That was a welcoming breath of fresh air for Lowry.

On the part of the Houston Rockets, they were also delighted to have had the opportunity to trade a young and promising point guard in exchange for cheap pieces. The Rockets, though a playoff team that season, were also trying to rebuild in a way, especially because center Yao Ming was frequently injured. An improving Aaron Brooks was their primary point guard, but they still hoped that Lowry could develop into something better.

Kyle Lowry would make his Rockets debut on February 20, 2009. He would score six points in about 15 minutes off the bench. Though Lowry would not play the same amount minutes he did when he was in Memphis, the best part of being in Houston was that the Rockets were winning. Lowry became a part of a winning culture when he was moved over to the Houston Rockets. It was only rightful because he was always a winner in high school and college.

Being with the Rockets made Kyle Lowry feel what it was like being on a team that was winning. Houston, banking on Yao Ming backed by the likes of Shane Battier and Ron Artest, were

41

on their way to one of the eight playoff spots in the tough Western Conference. Being with winners also influenced Lowry, who never had any successful veteran teammates in Memphis. Because of the winning culture in Houston and his admiration for his coach, Kyle Lowry's initial stay with the Rockets was a breeze for the developing point guard.

At the end of the regular season, Lowry's numbers did not fare well compared to his sophomore year in the NBA. He would norm 7.6 points, 2.5 rebounds, and 3.6 assists in a total of 77 games for both the Grizzlies and Rockets. Despite the drop in productivity, the important part for Lowry was that he was on a playoff team. The Houston managed to get a playoff spot as a middle-of-the-pack team in the West with their record of 53-29. Kyle Lowry was bound for the playoffs for the first time in three seasons.

Kyle Lowry's role in the playoffs did not change. He was still Brook's backup, but he proved that he was able to provide good minutes off the bench. In Game 1 of their matchup with the Portland Trailblazers, Lowry played 20 minutes of hard-nosed defense while scoring only two points on two attempts. He had his breakout playoff performance of 10 points in a loss in Game 2.

With the series tied one win apiece, Lowry provided quality minutes as a backup in Games 3 and 4. He had 8 points in 16 minutes of action in Game 3 to help the Rockets get a 2-1 series lead. Houston would pull away with a win in Game 4. Lowry scored only 4 points in that game, but had five rebounds and three steals. The Houston Rockets would end the series in six games. In Game 6, Kyle Lowry had 5 points, four rebounds, and three steals.

In the second round, Kyle Lowry was one of the key players off the bench when the Houston Rockets pushed the eventual champions Los Angeles Lakers team in their matchup. Matched up against the older and less athletic point guards of the Lakers, Lowry was able to produce well in limited minutes. He had 6 points and four rebounds in a Game 1 win in LA. The Lakers would bounce back in Game 2 where Lowry was 0 for seven from the floor.

Kyle Lowry, on a personal level, would bounce back in Game 3 in Houston. He had 8 points, four rebounds, and four assists in 22 minutes that game. However, the Lakers regained home-court advantage with that win. Not losing any confidence in himself, Lowry would have his then-best playoff performance in Game 4. He finished the 12-point win with 12 points, two rebounds, two assists, and two steals. With the series tied 2-2, LA would clobber Houston by 40 points in Game 5.

Facing possible elimination in Game 6, Kyle Lowry tried his best to do whatever he could to give a win to his team despite playing limited minutes. He would only see 15 minutes of action in that game. Nevertheless, he chipped in with 4 points and four assists in that outing to help force Game 7. Unfortunately, the Lakers would win by 19 points in the deciding final game of the series. In his first playoff appearance, Kyle Lowry averaged 5.3 points, 2.9 rebounds, and 2.5 assists in 13 total appearances.

First Full Season with the Houston Rockets

Nobody expected Kyle Lowry to become the primary point guard for the Rockets coming into the 2009-10 season. It was only right to think of such because Aaron Brooks was quickly developing into an accomplished starting point guard. But that did not stop Lowry from contributing to the Rockets in the best way he can.

Despite the fact that Lowry had to share minutes at the point guard spot with Brooks and the fact that his proportion of the time was only good for a bench player, his development was not hindered one bit. His confidence only grew as he began to trust

Adelman even more. In fact, he did not even bother playing behind Aaron Brooks because the system and the culture in Houston suited him.

On his part, Rick Adelman loved Lowry's presence in the team. He would go on to say that Kyle Lowry's constant attacking mentality was what he adored about the player.[iii] Though it was true that Kyle Lowry was an inconsistent shooter from anywhere beyond or inside the perimeter, he was such a good attacker that Adelman could not help but admire the spunk and the tenacity of his backup point guard.

In his first full season with the Houston Rockets, Kyle Lowry would get accustomed to life as a backup point guard. His attacking mentality, as well as his adjustment to the new system, was what made him an indispensable part of the team. As Adelman would put it, he was also a true point guard in every sense of the word because he had a sixth sense of knowing where his scorers were. He knew how to find leading scorer Kevin Martin, and he also knew where his spots were.[iii] This led Kyle Lowry to his best assisting seasons in four years in the NBA.

In just his first 20 games of the season, Kyle Lowry's assist numbers were top notch for a backup. He had five or more assists in nine of his first 20 games of the season. On top of that, he was also contributing well on the offensive end as he was also seeing himself scoring in double digits from time-to-time even while he was playing off the bench. The good thing about all of that was that the Rockets were still competing in an ultra-tough Western Conference setup.

On December 18, 2009, Kyle Lowry showed flashes of his future All-Star self. In that win against the Dallas Mavericks, the backup point guard played 38 minutes off the bench and showcased his talents on both ends of the floor. Lowry finished the game with a then career-high 26 points on top of the six rebounds, ten assists, and five steals he recorded. The so-called inconsistent shooter from the outside also drained three of his five attempts from downtown in that game.

After that career match, Lowry's minutes steadily increased game by game as Rick Adelman saw the potential within the young point guard. Adelman would sometimes employ a two point guard setup with Brooks and Lowry playing together in the backcourt so as to not hinder the development of both playmakers.

Just as Kyle Lowry was beginning to rise with the team, his development was momentarily derailed by an injury in February.

The injury kept him out for more than a month. After his return to the lineup, Lowry's minutes were inconsistent because he was reintegrating himself with the team. While Lowry was gone, the Rockets missed the services of their backup point guard. They were not performing as well as they had wanted to in the middle of the season.

Similar to his stint with the Grizzlies in his second season with the league, Kyle Lowry started to score more and began to look for his shots often in the tail end of the season because the Houston Rockets, though a team above .500 concerning wins, were already out of playoff contention. He would score in double digits in nine of his final 15 games of the season.

At the end of the 2009-10 season, Kyle Lowry averaged 9.1 points, 3.6 rebounds, and a then career-best 4.5 assists as Aaron Brooks' backup at the point guard position. He never started in the 68 appearances he made in the season and began to adore and love his role as one of the Rockets' best players off the bench. Despite the individual success, Lowry could not salvage the Rockets' season where the team was transitioning from the Yao and McGrady era. Houston finished the season with a 42-40 record and could not qualify for the playoffs just a year after pushing the 2009 champs to seven games.

Becoming a Starter

After an impressive 2009-10 season, Kyle Lowry was a hot commodity coming into the 2010 free agency period because of his ability to man the point as a backup. Other teams saw his potential as a starter for a squad that did not have an All-Star playmaker. And even if he was going to a team with an established point guard, Lowry could give any other playmaker a run for their money.

The team that pursued him the most coming into the 2010-11 season were the Cleveland Cavaliers, who were hoping to sign a quality player that could convince LeBron James to stay with the team. The Cavs had originally intended to draft Lowry back in 2006, but the point guard's alleged negative attitude turned them off. Seeing as how Lowry was a capable playmaker, they offered the point guard a $23 million four-year contract.

Lowry, realizing he could become a starter or key player with the Cavs, who might even go into the new season with James, agreed to the terms of the offered contract. He was about to become a Cavalier until the Rockets intervened. Since Kyle Lowry was a restricted free agent, the Houston Rockets could match any offer made on the point guard. They did so since Adelman and the organization believed what Lowry could do from that position. Kyle Lowry was staying with the Houston Rockets.

Kyle Lowry would go into the 2010-11 season as the backup to point guard Aaron Brooks, who was named the NBA's Most Improved Player during the 2009-10 season. There was no way that Lowry would steal the spotlight away from Brooks, who was just a few months off from a remarkable and impressive individual season performance.

Just when Lowry was going to stay a bench player for the rest of the season, Aaron Brooks went down with an ankle injury on November 6, 2010. Brooks would be sidelined from then on until December of the same year. Though injuries are always tragic, and though we could never wish it upon any professional athlete, it was the opportunity that Kyle Lowry was waiting for.

Kyle Lowry was promptly given the starting point guard spot after the Aaron Brooks injury. Lowry would own that role admirably not long after he became the designated point guard of the team. He would record his first point-assist double-double of the season on November 19 in a loss to the Toronto Raptors. He had 11 points and 12 assists in that game. In the next game, he recorded 13 points and six steals versus the Phoenix Suns before finishing a win against the Golden State Warriors with 14 points, seven rebounds, and ten assists.

As the season went on, Kyle Lowry's reputation as a competitor and capable starter became evident. On December 3, he would record a new career high in points. He had 28 points to go along with 12 assists in a win against the Memphis Grizzlies, his old team. The barrage would not stop there; he would score in double digits in the next three games. In one of those outings, he had 22 points, 12 assists, and six steals in a win over the Detroit Pistons. Lowry was finally showing his worth and his quality as a starter.

Kyle Lowry was also showcasing his ability to play both ends of the floor very well. He would have 17 points, five steals, and a career-best 18 assists in a win over the Memphis Grizzlies yet again on December 17. That game was part of a five-game double-digit scoring streak for Lowry. He would continue the season scoring well, making plays on an admirable level, and playing good solid defense on the other end.

Even as Aaron Brooks returned to the lineup in December, the starting point guard position was already Lowry's. Brooks was never able to replicate his 2009-10 magic because of the ankle injury he suffered. Because of that, he never got his starting spot back. The quality of play that Kyle Lowry was contributing in all facets of the game was partly to blame for that. While Brooks was the quicker and arguably better scorer, Lowry was the better rebounder, defender, and playmaker.

Not only was Kyle Lowry playing out of his mind when he finally took over the starting role, but his quality also gave the post-Yao Houston Rockets a chance of landing a playoff spot because they were regularly above the .500 mark throughout the season. The young point guard, at that early point in his career, was already proving his worth as a leader for a team that had a chance to contend for a postseason berth.

Lowry's rise to relevance made Brooks dispensable for the Rockets, who traded him over to the Phoenix Suns in February. By the time Brooks was traded to Phoenix, nobody else on the Rockets' roster could steal minutes away from Kyle Lowry. Nobody was going to stop him from further establishing himself as one of the most capable and quickly-developing point guards in the NBA. Adelman's trust in him only served to make the playmaker pour his heart out on the floor every single game.

As part of his tour of further proving himself to the rest of the league, Kyle Lowry would establish another new career high on February 16, 2011. He scored 36 points in that loss against the

Philadelphia 76ers. After that game, he would lead the Rockets to five straight wins, which included a 21-point, 11-assist effort from Lowry on March 1. In the very next match, Kyle Lowry recorded 24 points and 11 assists versus the Los Angeles Clippers.

In his final 20 games of the season, Lowry would score in double digits in 19 straight outings except for the last scheduled bout for the Rockets. Kyle Lowry had a lot of impressive games during that stretch. He scored 32 points in a loss to the Suns on March 8. He then had his first career triple-double in a win over the Utah Jazz on March 20 while leading his team to what would become a five-game winning streak. In that win, he had 28 points, 11 rebounds, ten assists, and three steals. On top of scoring, Kyle Lowry was also passing the ball at a high rate and defending the other end impressively for his size at the point guard spot.

At the end of his first season as the designated starting point guard for the Houston Rockets, Kyle Lowry averaged 13.5 points, 4.1 rebounds, 6.7 assists, and 1.4 steals. Those were all then-career-highs. On top of that, Lowry was also making 38% of the 4.6 shots he attempted from beyond the arc every game. Not only was he improving overall as a player, but he was also becoming a deadly marksman from the outside. Despite the personal improvements from Lowry that season, the Rockets would miss the playoffs again after finishing the season with a record of 43-39.

Adelman Out, Clashing with McHale

Realizing they had to go separate ways and that Adelman was not up for the job of rebuilding the Houston Rockets, the organization replaced Rick with the legendary big man and multiple-time NBA champion Kevin McHale. Unfortunately for the Rockets, the decision of replacing Adelman with McHale did not sit well with their starting point guard.

Kyle Lowry favored Rick Adelman as a coach. He was the first NBA head coach that had earned Lowry's trust because, in turn, he believed in the point guard back. Adelman believed in Lowry's abilities as a player. That was what made him endearing to Kyle Lowry. He was already comfortable with Rick Adelman. The transition to McHale was not as easy for him.[iii]

For Lowry, McHale was a whole new, different coach. He was stricter than Adelman while his offensive and defensive schemes were a lot different. The fact that he was already comfortable with Adelman's system was what made the change so difficult for him. Nevertheless, Kyle Lowry was still the

Rockets' best point guard, and he was still up for the job with McHale.

Lowry would open the lockout-shortened 2011-12 season with 20 points, seven rebounds, and 12 assists in a loss to the Orlando Magic on December 26, 2011. Despite the opening day loss, Lowry would admirably and slowly lead the Rockets back to contention. He would do it not with his scoring, but by playing every facet of the game well. On December 31, he would only score 2 points on 0 out of 6 from the field. He had 18 assists and made life difficult for the opposing point guards of the Atlanta Hawks in that win.

From January 11 to 23 of 2012, Kyle Lowry had one of the best stretches of his career. He would score 22 points in a loss to the San Antonio Spurs in the first game of that stretch. From then on, he would lead his Houston Rockets to seven straight wins while putting up impressive stats. He would have 25 points, seven rebounds, and nine assists after that loss to the Spurs before having a stat line of 33 points, eight rebounds, and nine assists in an overtime win against the Portland Trailblazers. He would score in double digits in all seven straight wins before capping it off with a triple-double performance of 16 points, ten rebounds, and ten assists in a win over the Minnesota Timberwolves.

From the looks of things after that stretch of wins for the Houston Rockets, and after starting the season considerably well, it seemed like the team was back to playoff contention and relevance in the Western Conference. But things quickly turned sour for the Rockets and, in turn, for Kyle Lowry as well.

Kevin McHale would suddenly find a gem in backup point guard Goran Dragic. The rise of Dragic meant that McHale was slowly decreasing Lowry's minutes at the point guard spot for the former. The decline of his role did not sit well for Kyle Lowry. In turn, the Rockets were also suddenly becoming inconsistent as a team regarding wins.

Despite all that, Kyle Lowry tried his best to steer the Rockets' ship to the right direction. Lowry was playing at a borderline All-Star level that season while trying to make the Rockets competitive again. Though he was not an All-Star, it seemed as if he was on the right track to getting there. He even had good performances throughout the trying times of the Rockets that season.

Though the Houston Rockets did not have a legitimate superstar that could shoulder the burdens of the team, they were competing hard every single game thanks to the tenacity of their starting point guard. Lowry, though he did not lead his team in scoring, was the main reason why the Rockets were not a laughing stock that season, though they were essentially rebuilding. Because of his play and leadership qualities, many believed he should have been an All-Star.

Lowry's near-star quality of playing the game would resurface from time-to-time. On February 19, Kyle Lowry put up 32 points and nine assists in a win over the Utah Jazz. What made that performance impressive for Lowry was that he made 7 out of 8 of his three-pointers as he continued to shed his reputation of being a subpar shooter from the outside. He would score in double digits in the next three games while helping his team win four straight bouts.

However, early in March, Kyle Lowry would get sidelined because of a bacterial infection. Similar to how Lowry himself took advantage of Brooks' injury back in the 2009-10 season, Goran Dragic filled in excellently for the injured starting point guard. Dragic, who was arguably the better scorer and more electrifying player made himself endearing to McHale and the Houston faithful. He made Lowry dispensable.

When Lowry got back from injury, Kevin McHale would play him off the bench for the improving Goran Dragic. He would never regain his starting role as the season ended. In fact, his minutes were dropping quickly while Dragic's role only continued to increase game after game.

At the end of the 2011-12 season, Kyle Lowry averaged then-career highs of 14.3 points and 4.5 rebounds to go along with 6.6 assists and 1.6 steals. As he would put it himself, he was very successful under Kevin McHale. Unfortunately, he was uncomfortable with the system that McHale implemented with the Rockets, who would miss the playoffs yet again despite winning more than half of their games.

Kelvin Sampson, one of McHale's assistants, knew what was up with the point guard. He thought that Lowry never actually accepted the change in coaching. As history would show, Lowry has always had a difficulty in learning how to accept change after trusting his old coach for so long. But Kyle Lowry was never comfortable with the way McHale did things. He would even confront the head coach about their differences in ideals. Lowry was a very confrontational player and one that wanted to do things his way.[iii]

Sampson would go on to say that he did not think that there was something wrong with the way McHale was handling things. What he thought was that Lowry just did not like that Adelman was replaced. It did not matter who was replacing him. The fact that did not sit well with Lowry was that the coach he trusted was gone. Because of this and how quick Dragic was rising, Kyle Lowry was probably on his way out of Houston.

Trade to Toronto

The Houston Rockets realized that they could get nowhere with how Lowry and McHale did not see eye-to-eye. Realizing that Goran Dragic was the point guard that could help them usher in a new era, the Rockets decided to trade away their former starting point guard to the Toronto Raptors to clear some cap space and acquire draft picks.

Initially, the trade did not sit well with Kyle Lowry. He knew that the Toronto Raptors had plans of signing veteran former All-Star and two-time MVP Steve Nash, who was a native of Canada. The plan was that they would make the trade for Lowry and then sign Nash, who would in turn mentor the former until his retirement.[iii]

On his part, Lowry did not want to wait at least two more seasons to take over the team. Although he admired Steve Nash and what the two-time MVP had accomplished, he did not want to play behind the veteran. He wanted to be the leading man and told the Raptors that he did not like their plans. However, Toronto proceeded with the trade for Lowry, but could not sign

Steve Nash. Things, nonetheless, ended well for Kyle Lowry in his second fresh start in the NBA.

In Toronto, Kyle Lowry was happy to be back playing with Rudy Gay, who was acquired midseason that year and was one of his closest friends back when they were suiting up together in Memphis. Lowry knew his friend's tendencies on the floor, and also knew how to find the athletic swingman. What he also liked about playing for Toronto was that nobody was out there on the roster getting minutes from him. The only other capable point guard was Jose Calderon who, despite being an excellent passer, was not nearly as good as Lowry in every other facet of the game.

Calderon was one of the best players at passing the ball. Whenever you wanted a point guard that would always make it a point to look for his teammates, Jose Calderon was the guy you would want to have on your roster. As good as Calderon was at running an offense, then Raptors general manager Bryan Colangelo wanted a point guard to usher in a bright future for Toronto.[iii] Calderon, at his age, could not do it. Only Lowry could.

Despite the trust given to him by the entire Raptors organization, Kyle Lowry could not get wins for the team early in the season.

But that did not stop him from putting up terrific numbers. He made his Raptors debut on October 31, 2012, in a loss to the Indiana Pacers. He had 21 points, seven rebounds, eight assists, and five steals that game. Lowry would then score at least 20 points in the next two games while also maintaining rebounding and supporting numbers of more than five a game.

After a quick and successful start to the season, Kyle Lowry would be injured in his fourth game of the year. He would only score 2 points in about 17 minutes in that loss to the Oklahoma City Thunder. Because of his injury, the Raptors turned to veteran Jose Calderon for point guard services. But even with Calderon manning the point, the Raptors could not get any semblance of traction early in the season.

When Lowry returned late in November, he quickly regained the starting spot from Calderon. He also swiftly went back to where he left off. Lowry was putting up good numbers all over the stat sheet. The 6'0" point guard was scoring and attacking at will while also grabbing tons of rebounds for his size. His best game at that juncture of the season came in a loss to the Sacramento Kings. Lowry had 34 points, five rebounds, and 11 assists in that match.

Shortly after coming back from injury, Kyle Lowry would get sidelined due to injury yet again. He would come back late in December when the year was all but coming to an end. At that point, head coach Dwane Casey gave him bench duties for Jose Calderon. Though Kyle Lowry did his best to contribute from that role, he never did as much damage to opposing teams as he did when he was starting.

Again, Lowry was not happy about it. The Toronto Raptors traded a first-round draft pick for him, yet they were not willing to play him to his full potential. Kyle Lowry thought it was an insult to his abilities. It caused him to rethink his development as a player. He was almost an All-Star in his final year in Houston, but in Toronto, he was back to playing bench minutes.[iii]

Because of that experience, Kyle Lowry dreaded the idea of resigning with the team when his contract ended in two seasons. Lowry was back to where he started when he first entered the league. He was back to doing bench duties for a struggling franchise. It seemed that all the experience and work he had put in the past seasons were going down the drain.

The sad part about all that for Lowry was that he was seeing his team lose badly almost every night while he was sitting on the bench unable to do anything about it. Calderon was a capable point guard in his right, but he did not have the tools to steer the rebuilding Toronto Raptors to the right course. That role should have gone to Kyle Lowry, who was arguably the better all-around point guard.

Nevertheless, Kyle Lowry would get his starting spot back when the Toronto Raptors decided to trade away Calderon. It was the same trade that had brought Rudy Gay over to the Raptors. With Calderon gone, Lowry took back the starting point guard position. This time, his efforts were drawn towards finding his high-scoring teammates and towards playing tough defense against opposing point guards.

Since acquiring Rudy Gay in the trade that moved Jose Calderon, Kyle Lowry never scored more than 20 points in a single game. Whether that was right or wrong for the Raptors was up for analysts and coaches to decide. What mattered was that Lowry adjusted his game for better and more athletic scorers. He was becoming more of a point guard than he had ever been in his career.

While the Rudy Gay trade did not change the fate of the struggling Raptors that season, it made the franchise hopeful and confident. The additional talent and athleticism would help the team in the seasons to come. And with Kyle Lowry back to his job of distributing the ball at the starting point guard spot, the franchise had no reason to worry.

Kyle Lowry averaged 11.6 points, 4.7 rebounds, 6.4 assists, and 1.4 steals in his first season with the Toronto Raptors. Though his stats were down compared to his final two seasons with the Rockets, he seemed to be a better fit for a Raptors team that was seeking to become contenders in the Eastern Conference in future seasons. They would, however, miss the 2013 playoffs because of a subpar record.

Rising with the Raptors, Return to the Playoffs

One of the best things in roster history happened to the Toronto Raptors when Masai Ujiri replaced Colangelo as the general manager of the team. Ujiri would go on to learn more about the players he was going to work with for the next few seasons. The most discussed player was, of course, Kyle Lowry.

Everything Ujiri heard about Lowry was outside of basketball. Nobody was complaining about the point guard's skills. He could score, shoot, pass, rebound, and defend. He was one of the best competitors out there. But the problem was that he always challenged authority. He did not want to be coached.[iii]

Because of what he heard, Ujiri proceeded to challenge Kyle Lowry. The problem he had with Lowry was controllable. Compared to other guys that could not score, shoot, defend, or rebound, every problem surrounding Lowry could be remedied. He believed that Lowry had the abilities that could put any other point guard to shame if utilized correctly.

Ujiri would talk to Lowry before the season started. He told his playmaker that he believed that Kyle Lowry had all the talent in the world to become an elite player in the NBA. The general manager would also tell the point guard to fix his attitude if he wanted to be a player worth the max offer. Talent is useless if not coupled with the right attitude and mindset. Instead of being offended, Kyle Lowry took it as a challenge.

One other person that challenged Kyle Lowry to do better was former All-Star and NBA champion Chauncey Billups. Billups also had a reputation of going against authority. He did not start his career well, but exploded in Detroit. It would take him nine seasons to become an All-Star. Billups told Lowry about his similar experiences and also challenged the latter to become better than he was. Lowry would look up to Billups from then on.[iii]

With no other point guard on the roster capable of matching up to his skills and competitive edge, Kyle Lowry was the designated starter of the Toronto Raptors and was arguably their best overall player coming into the 2013-14 season. At the start of the season, he did his best to make his scorers DeRozan and Gay happy by making it a point to give them open looks. However, the DeRozan-Gay experiment did not work well, and the Raptors were 6-12 early in the season. Gay was moved over to the Kings, and from then on, Kyle Lowry looked like a man possessed.

Ujiri would go on to say that the Rudy Gay experiment did not work out because there was no chemistry between the Raptors' top three players. Everyone needed the ball in their hands for them to become productive. There was no spacing or flow to the game. What the Raptors needed was someone to make plays for them. They did not need three guys trying to do things their way. The Gay trade was what got them going.

Since the Raptors moved Rudy Gay, Lowry suddenly did his best to find shots for himself. Nobody else was going to score. He took it upon himself to become one of the best scorers in the team while maintaining his penchant for doing everything else at a high level. Kyle Lowry was consistently putting up at least 20 points a night without compromising his ability to rebound, assist, and defend night in and night out. The best thing about it was that the Raptors were rising with him.

Unfortunately for Lowry, he was also the subject of trade talks at that juncture of the season. Distel, his good friend from way back in high school, said that Lowry was shaken about the reports saying that the New York Knicks were highly interested in his services. He was about to go to New York in the middle of December 2013 before the deal was abandoned at the very last minute.[i] Though the near-move affected him, Lowry came out of that experience as a better player.

A more mature Kyle Lowry would talk with young and athletic swingman DeMar DeRozan, who was quickly developing into Toronto's deadliest scorer. He discussed his future with DeRozan as his backcourt mate. He told the athletic swingman that they were going to be a winning combination no matter what.

In turn, DeMar also told Kyle what he wanted to happen. He said that he wanted Lowry to be on the same page as him concerning their hunger to win. DeRozan told Lowry that both of their futures in Toronto would be secured if both of them played their best. The swingman would tell his point guard that they needed to pull off a playoff push to convince the organization that their duo was worth trusting. The backcourt duo would become closer after that.

Lowry then went over to Dwane Casey to try and let the strategist understand his point of view about the Raptors' situation. Casey had a different idea of what a point guard was and how a playmaker should be on the floor. Unfortunately, his beliefs did not coincide with how Kyle Lowry played. The good thing was that both player and coach learned how to adjust and trust one another after talking and respecting each other's differences.

Casey would understand that there were qualities in Lowry's personality that you could never take away. He was tough, competitive, hardheaded, and emotional at times. But those aspects were what made him better. Taking away some of his qualities would change Kyle Lowry into something he was not. All of this made Casey reminisce about a player he once helped mentor.

Dwane Casey had the opportunity to coach Gary Payton as an assistant back in the 90's when he was working under George Karl on the Seattle SuperSonics. Casey saw how Karl coached Payton. Gary Payton was always one of the most competitive players the league has ever seen. In line with that, he talked tough and was also hardheaded at times. But George Karl allowed Gary Payton to be himself. That was something Casey wanted to do with Lowry, who mirrored Payton's style and personality.

After that episode, the Toronto Raptors suddenly turned their season around. They would begin to win more games than what the fans and the organization were accustomed to. Of course, in the middle of all that was Kyle Lowry, who exploded onto the scene after nearly being traded to the Knicks. Lowry would score in double digits in all of the games he played from December 14 to January 20, 2014. He had four double-doubles in that span while leading the Raptors to a 12-7 record in that 19-game span.

As the season continued, Kyle Lowry seemed like a player that could make the All-Star team. He was doing everything for the Raptors. Lowry was piling up the statistics while also leading his team to a record that could give the Raptors a playoff berth. In line with his penchant for filling up the stat sheet, he had a triple-double on January 24 in a win against the Philadelphia 76ers. He had 18 points, ten rebounds, and 13 assists in that game. Two days later, he had back-to-back games of scoring at least 30 points in wins against the Brooklyn Nets and Orlando Magic.

As he tried to convince people around the league that he was worth an All-Star spot, Kyle Lowry would have three consecutive double-doubles in assists and scoring in the middle of February. All three games were wins. Not only was he becoming a leader for the Toronto Raptors, he was becoming an ideal point guard for Dwane Casey and an elite point guard in the league.

Despite putting up terrific statistics night in and night out and despite leading the team to a good record in the middle of the season, Kyle Lowry was not selected as an All-Star. Dwane Casey said that he believed that no other point guard in the East was better than Lowry at that point in the season.[i] True enough, no other point guard played both ends of the floor at a higher level than Kyle Lowry did. On top of all that, he was even making the Raptors contenders in their conference and the top team in their division.

On his part, Kyle Lowry did not take it too personally that he was not selected as an All-Star that season. He was never the type of player that relied on individual goals. Lowry believed that being an All-Star was something good for a person's legacy and was something to be proud of. But it was not something he was looking forward to that season. Lowry said that being a winner and putting up wins was more important than personal

69

goals.[i] All-Star appearances and other personal achievements usually come with wins. Winning was what Lowry would focus on as the season progressed into the second half.

The Toronto Raptors would power into the end of the season with an improved record of 48-34. The Raptors were the third seed coming into the playoffs, and they were also able to beat out the Knicks and Nets for the division title. And since almost trading Kyle Lowry in December, the Raptors won more games than any other team in the Eastern Conference.[iii]

In the middle of all that was their star point guard, who averaged career bests of 17.9 points, 4.7 rebounds, and 7.4 assists. He also shot a career-best 38% from the three-point line while making 2.4 shots per game from that distance. It was during that season that Kyle Lowry proved he was an elite point guard in all aspects despite not making the All-Star or an All-NBA team. Kyle Lowry's offense was perfect and he could make shots from anywhere on the floor. He also rebounded and assisted at high rates. And for his size, he was an elite defender. If there was a player that could usher in a new future for Toronto in that season and subsequent years, it was Kyle Lowry.

For the first time in five seasons and the first time since 2009, Kyle Lowry was back to the playoffs. However, things were already a lot different since then. In 2009, he had just joined the Houston Rockets and was the backup point guard to Aaron Brooks. He was not the leader of his team back then. But in 2014, he was arguably the best player that the Toronto Raptors had. He was not a backup and was not just a starter. Lowry was the leader and barometer of the Toronto Raptors. The Raptors could only get as far as Kyle Lowry could take them.

In their return trip to the playoffs, the Toronto Raptors were going up against a veteran-laded Brooklyn Nets team. Against a bigger and more established point guard in Deron Williams, Kyle Lowry held his own. He finished with 22 points, seven rebounds, and eight assists that game. However, the Raptors fell in that opening bout. In a less stellar performance in Game 2, Lowry was somehow able to lead his team to tie the series up.

In Game 3 in Brooklyn, the Raptors once again fought the Nets toe-to-toe for the series lead. Unfortunately for Kyle Lowry in that match, he did not see it through to the end and struggled to contain the Nets' guards without fouling. He would foul out of the game while Brooklyn took the series lead. From then on, Kyle Lowry would show his quality as a leader.

In Game 4, Kyle Lowry would shed away his penchant for playmaking for him to put on a good show on both offense and defense. He would score 22 points on a good solid offensive effort while also playing hard defense on the opposing point guards of Brooklyn. Both Deron Williams and Shaun Livingston were limited to a combined 19-point effort on 7 out of 19 shooting from the field. In a high-scoring Game 5, Kyle Lowry was once again on full display. He made 6 of his nine attempts from the three-point line to score a new playoff high 36 points. Once again, he also limited the Nets' point guard duo to a poor offensive night. The Toronto Raptors led 3-2 in the series after those two wins.

The Raptors only had one more game to win before proceeding to the second round of the playoffs. They had two chances to close the series out. In Game 6 in Brooklyn, Toronto would squander their first chance to beat the Nets after Kyle Lowry was limited to only 11 points on 4 out of 16 shooting while Williams was able to exact revenge by scoring 23 points.

With the series tied 3-3, the Toronto Raptors were back home to try and beat the Brooklyn Nets in a historic Game 7. Throughout the epic match, neither team gave an edge. Both the Raptors and the Nets fought each other to a standstill. It took until the final play to decide who was going to the second round.

With the Raptors down by one point, they would go to their leader Kyle Lowry. Lowry would proceed to attack the basket for a possible game-winning shot near the basket. However, veteran forward Paul Pierce would thwart his efforts by blocking the potential game-winner. The block took away the Toronto Raptors' chances of proceeding to the second round of the playoffs that season.

First All-Star Season

After the Toronto Raptors' season had ended with that block by Paul Pierce on Kyle Lowry, the star point guard had all the reasons and talent to command a good contract offer from any team when he came into free agency. He had all the confidence in the world as one of the fastest rising playmakers in the NBA. Masai Ujiri was right in saying that Lowry only needed to fix his attitude for him to command a max offer.

In the free agency period, Kyle Lowry was a hot commodity, but not as a bench guy or as a role player. He was a legitimate starter and borderline All-Star that could impact any team on any given night. He would get offers from the Miami Heat, and surprisingly, the Houston Rockets, which was the same team that had given up on him two seasons ago.

On his part, Kyle Lowry would go on to say that he was open to leaving the Toronto Raptors for one of the teams that were courting him. Like a true point guard, Lowry stated that he looked at the advantages and disadvantages of every step he would make from then on. He looked at the salary cap situation of every team that courted him. On top of that, he even went on to watch who were going to be free agents in a few years as he was predicting his chances of playing with top notch talent in the coming seasons.

The first team he met during that period were the Houston Rockets. As a sign of his maturity and growth as a leader and player, Lowry would first apologize to Rockets then head coach Kevin McHale. After apologizing, McHale probably did not say the right words when he told Lowry that the playmaker would have to regain the trust of the coaches again if he decided to go to Houston. That turned Lowry off as he worked so hard to earn the trust of his coaches in Toronto and positioned himself into the best spot in his career.

However, Kyle Lowry was still interested in signing with the Rockets because of the team's talented players and because they were in the position of possibly signing a marquee free agent in future seasons. The Houston Rockets held off any plans of signing Lowry until bigger names such as LeBron James or Chris Bosh decided where they wanted to go.

In the meantime, Masai Ujiri would meet with Kyle Lowry to convince him to stay in Toronto. He told his point guard that he had what it took to take the Raptors to the next level. In Toronto, Lowry was not going to be the third guy of another big three on another team. He was going to the sole leader in Toronto. The Raptors were going to be his team, and he was not going to play second fiddle.[i]

When Ujiri told him this, Kyle Lowry suddenly remembered his days back in Philadelphia. In 2001 when he was but a high school kid, Lowry saw how people from all over the state drove all the way to Philadelphia to watch Allen Iverson lead his underdog 76ers team against a powerhouse Los Angeles Lakers team in the NBA Finals.

Allen Iverson back then was a one-man show for Philadelphia. He was the only guy that could do the job on the 76ers team. Despite being named the 2001 MVP, he was an underdog facing a team that would soon form a dynasty in the league. Iverson was the single icon that kept the city of Philadelphia united in their battle against the Lakers. Lowry wanted that. He wanted to be the guy that could unite the city of Toronto when he would someday get a chance to play in the Finals. Because of that, he decided to stay with the Toronto Raptors for a four-year contract worth $48 million, which was double what he commanded in his last free agency trip.

Coming into the 2014-15 season with their leader back in the lineup, the Toronto Raptors had another high chance to get a good seeding in the playoffs. Why not? They had a competent top scorer in the name of DeMar DeRozan. Their other key starters Jonas Valanciunas and Amir Johnson had also developed into capable players in their respective positions. Moreover, their bench was competitive with guys like Patrick Patterson, Terrence Ross, Greivis Vasquez, and offseason acquisition Lou Williams backing up the starters.

However, the Eastern Conference was also getting tougher and tougher after going through a massive change in the free agency period. The Cleveland Cavaliers were a clear favorite after signing James and acquiring Kevin Love. With a healthy Derrick Rose returning to Chicago, the Bulls were also going to be competitive among perennial contenders such as Indiana and Miami. Despite being one year better and one year more mature, the Raptors were going to have to work harder to get a good playoff spot.

Nevertheless, Kyle Lowry believed that he and his team had what it took to take the game to everybody else in the Eastern Conference setup. He said that they were not the coolest-looking team compared to the other contenders in the East. On his part, Lowry was not the greatest looking point guard in the NBA. He had a strong game that was predicated on his pit bull style of doing things. But he got the job done every single night.

In the first 20 games of the 2014-15 season, Kyle Lowry helped his Toronto Raptors get the job done. They were 15-5 at that early juncture of the season. In that span, Kyle Lowry seemed better than he ever was. In just his fifth game of the season, he scored 35 points, which were followed up by a triple-double versus the Washington Wizards. Because of that performance, Lowry became the all-time leader in triple-doubles in Raptors history. Much later early in December, he put up a career-high 39 points against the Utah Jazz. All three great performances were wins.

It was in December of that season when Kyle Lowry was on full display. That month, Lowry led the Toronto Raptors to an 11-4 win-loss record, which also included six straight wins for the team. Lowry also had two games of scoring at least 30 points and also had six double-double outings. He averaged 22.3 points, 4.2 rebounds, and 8.9 assists in December. Because of his performance, he was named December's Eastern Conference Player of the Month.

Not only was Kyle Lowry playing at a personal high at that part of his career, his popularity was also at an all-time high. His name was regularly mentioned among the top point guards not only in the East, but the whole league as well. On top of all that, Kyle Lowry was so popular that fans voted him into the Eastern Conference All-Star squad as a starter. For the first time in his career, Kyle Lowry was an All-Star and a starter at that. The name he passed to become an All-Star starter was none other than Dwyane Wade, who was a future Hall of Fame guard himself.

After nine seasons in the NBA, Kyle Lowry finally saw his name mentioned among the top players in the NBA. Nearing 29 years old, Lowry was at the age when not a lot of players were becoming All-Stars for the first time. But he finally made the cut after early stints as a backup in Memphis and Houston. It was only in Toronto that he finally blossomed into an elite player after head coach Dwane Casey gave him the reigns.

Compared to other All-Stars, Lowry's emergence as one of the best players in the NBA was a bumpy ride. He was not Michael Jordan, Shaquille O'Neal, or LeBron James, who all became

All-Stars in no time. Lowry was not Kawhi Leonard, Paul George, or Jimmy Butler, who all needed only a few years to develop to become some of the best players in the NBA. His was a nine-year journey to stardom that started with setback after setback and criticisms about his attitude in how he regularly clashed with authority. But, like he always did, Kyle Lowry made the NBA All-Star team his way—by being a winner.

Lowry, though it took him nine seasons to get to one of the pinnacles of success in the NBA, should not be ashamed of how he got to become an All-Star. He faced numerous and countless humiliating moments and criticism early in his career. The Memphis Grizzlies chose to put their hopes on lottery pick Mike Conley as their point guard for the future. Conley, unlike Lowry, has yet to become an All-Star. In Houston, he suffered through a season struggling to mesh with head coach Kevin McHale before being traded in the offseason.

Through his journey to All-Stardom, Kyle Lowry has seen his share of clashes with authority and improved relationships with leaders. He has seen how different leaders and coaches handle their teams and players. His volatile nature also allowed him to get a glimpse of how his immaturity affected his game and the play of his team.[v]

It was all the difficulties and tribulations that helped Kyle Lowry develop into an All-Star. He has seen how his past teams struggled throughout the season, and he has also experienced how frustrating it was to play off the bench for more hyped and experienced point guards. But he never gave up any of those times. He continued to hustle and compete every single night. But, with the help of his coaches and authority figures in Toronto, all those experiences helped Lowry see the error of his ways and to mature as a player. He would never take those moments for granted one bit.

Averaging 18.8 points and 7.4 assists entering the All-Star break, Kyle Lowry was not alone in his bid for a spot at the midseason classic. The whole country of Canada, as well as the entire Toronto organization, were in full support for the Raptors' best player since Chris Bosh. The prime minister and well-known celebrities helped Lowry gain some recognition and traction as an All-Star starter for the very first time in his career.[i]

While he was doing things his way to get the trust and recognition of his coaches, Lowry was also getting the adoration and love of Toronto supporters and NBA fans in general. For the first time in his career, Kyle Lowry felt at home in a city he could not even wait to get out of when he first got there. The first-time All-Star would score 10 points, dish out eight assists, and steal four possessions in the midseason classic held in New York.

Throughout the individual success of Kyle Lowry that season, he still believed that he was not the best star in his team. In fact, he was happier for DeMar DeRozan when the high-flying swingman was named an All-Star in 2014. Even Casey recognizes that Lowry never wanted to be known as the best player on his team. All he wanted to do was run his squad and to lead them to wins.

Dwane Casey saw how Kyle Lowry worked harder than everyone else on the Raptors team. That was what he was always preaching to his team. He wanted his leaders and best players to lead by example, not in statistics, but in heart, competitiveness, and work ethic. Lowry personifies all of those qualities. That was what made Casey believe in his point guard as much as he had believed in Gary Payton in Seattle all those years ago.[v] Kyle Lowry would always be the one to chase after loose balls and to attack bigger opposing players. He brought the competitive edge and the ferocity that inspired all of his other teammates.

The fact that Lowry played hard night in and night out was what made him the most valuable Raptor in the organization. He did not lead the team in scoring, nor did he have the gaudiest numbers in the NBA. But he got the job done, and he gave wins to his team by playing the role of a pit bull each game. Even backcourt mate DeMar DeRozan recognized how Lowry's passionate play boosted the positivity of his team.

But the All-Star appearance for Kyle Lowry was just the beginning of his career. Nine years into the NBA, nobody would expect Lowry to continue to rise or even play at the level he was playing in that season. Kyle Lowry's competitive nature and hunger to win would not allow him to stagnate, even as aged into his 30's. His game was never predicated on his athletic abilities. He always got his numbers and wins by competing harder than everyone else and by constantly believing that he could conquer all despite his small stature.

But it was never Lowry's top goal to make the All-Star team. Kyle Lowry, being a winner, wanted more than anything else to take his team deep into the playoffs. He never cared about anything else in basketball other than winning. Lowry was always about the wins, ever since he was part of a winning culture in high school. He took that mentality to Villanova and all the way to the NBA despite experiencing losing seasons in

Memphis and Houston. Winning was all that he was going to care about as the Toronto Raptors looked to solidify their playoff positioning heading into the second half of the season.

Despite the hype and excitement surrounding the Toronto Raptors and their leader, who became an All-Star for the very first time in his career, the team would see rough stretches after the midseason break. After beating the conference-leading Atlanta Hawks by 25 points in their first game back from the All-Star break, they would lose nine of their next ten games. Lowry was inactive due to injury in three of those games.

The Toronto Raptors' struggles would continue as the season progressed and neared its end. A lot of those struggles had to do with Lowry's health at that juncture of the season. Kyle Lowry would experience a myriad of injury combinations which included back, hamstring, and hand ailments. But his lower back was what was killing him the most.[vi]

And even if Lowry was actively part of the roster, many believed that it was his stamina and conditioning that was hurting his game and his team's chances at a high playoff spot. Kyle Lowry, despite being at the peak of his career and after making the All-Star team for the first time, was pudgy and out of shape in the second half of the NBA season.

Even though it was his big physique that allowed him to attack and bully softer guards, it was what held him down. It seemed that all the carrying he had to do in the first half of the season took a toll on his body and stamina as he slowed down his productivity and as his health was failing him when the season was about to end. Lowry's health and conditioning were a doom spell for the Raptors entering the playoffs.

Without their star point guard for most of the second half of the season, the Toronto Raptors struggled to win games by simply banking on backup Greivis Vasquez. Lowry was what they needed. Unfortunately, the All-Star playmaker was not in the shape or the best health to give his all to his team, who were reeling and struggling to get momentum as the postseason neared.

Despite all the wear and tear, Kyle Lowry, in his first ever All-Star season, averaged 17.8 points, 4.7 rebounds, 6.8 assists, and 1.6 steals. Lowry was playing out of his mind entering the All-Star break before his injuries, and his conditioning slowed him down in the second half of the season. Despite all that, Lowry was still able to lead his Toronto Raptors to the fourth seed in the East with a record of 49-33.

In the first round of the playoffs, Kyle Lowry and his Raptors were set to face the Washington Wizards led by fellow All-Star starter John Wall. Facing the bigger and more athletic Wall would prove to be a challenge for Lowry. But the biggest hurdle and wall he would have to climb over was the burden of carrying an injured back and fatigued body coming into that matchup.

In Game 1 of that series, it would seem that Kyle Lowry's injuries and conditioning problems had caught up to him in the playoffs. The All-Star point guard was limited to a miserable night on the offensive end of the floor. Though he would put the clamps on Wall, who had a bad shooting night, Lowry was 2 for ten from the floor and could only muster up 7 points, eight rebounds, and four assists in 34 minutes when his team lost the opening bout.

After doing a terrific job on John Wall in Game 1 despite losing that outing, Kyle Lowry was embarrassingly outplayed in Game 2. Not only did he allow his opposing matchup to finish the game with a stat line of 26 points and 17 assists, he also could not match the energy and effort that John Wall put up that night. Lowry was merely 3 out of 10 from the floor and finished with only 6 points, two rebounds, and four assists in what was a consecutive poor performance for an All-Star starter. Again, the

85

Raptors lost that game and were headed to a 0-2 deficit as the series moved over to Washington.

Looking at Lowry's stat line and performances in Games 1 and 2 were not indicative of how an All-Star starter should be playing and contributing in the playoffs. Even backup guards Lou Williams and Greivis Vasquez were having a better postseason than their team leader. Things would not change in Game 3 when Lowry once again allowed Wall to impose his will on the offensive end while only contributing 15 points on a miserable 5 out of 22 from the field. After Game 3, the Toronto Raptors were down 0-3 and were virtually out of the running in the playoffs.

Not to be outdone and not willing to back down against the Wizards despite facing the insurmountable odds of coming back from a 0-3 series deficit, Kyle Lowry would put up his best performance of the series. In that game, Lowry did not allow his opposing All-Star point guard to score as much as he had the last two games. On top of that, he was even had his best shooting clip of the series going 8 out of 15 from the floor. He ended the game with 21 points, eight rebounds, and four assists.

Unfortunately, that performance came too late. The Raptors were already down 0-3. Because of that, the rest of the team already had virtually given up on their chances of moving on to the next round. On top of that, the Washington Wizards were already intent on finishing the series. The Raptors would allow their opponents to score at will without even putting up an effort on the defensive end. Lowry's best performance of the series was wasted in what was a 31-point blowout loss.

At the end of that miserable and embarrassing four-game series loss to the Washington Wizards, Kyle Lowry averaged only 12.3 points, 5.5 rebounds, 4.8 steals, and 1.3 assists. From those numbers alone, Lowry was indeed limited by his injuries and his alleged conditioning problems. What was more glaring was the fact that he shot only 31.6% from the floor. His performance in that series could never give justice to the stellar regular season he was having before his physical problems. But, in any case, it was evident that the Toronto Raptors could only go as far as Kyle Lowry could bring them.

Slimming Down, Improved Conditioning, Breaking Through to the Eastern Conference Finals

Coming into the 2015-16 NBA season, Kyle Lowry knew that his poor performance in the series against the Washington Wizards was what had caused them to lose four games in the first round. A myriad of injuries and his subpar conditioning were factors for that miserable output. He was not in the best physical shape of his life in that series. Lowry had been nursing a back injury that had him reeling in pain throughout the final half of that 82-game stretch. On top of that, he was not in the best shape of his life.

The worst part was that everyone knew and thought that Lowry's health was what had them reeling to the lower-seeded Wizards in that series. Forward Patrick Patterson said that Kyle should have been Kyle in that series. But he also recognized that Lowry was not himself because of the injuries.[vii]

Even Dwane Casey was well aware of how badly Kyle Lowry played that series. Casey would say that his star point guard was dealing with rust on top of all the injuries he had suffered in their quest to get a good seeding. Lowry barely played for the Raptors in the second half of the season. Because of that, the All-Star had problems of getting back to game shape even assuming arguendo that his health was back to a hundred percent.[vii]

Of course, Lowry was not spared from criticism because of that miserable series against the Wizards. As how many predicted when Lowry received a lucrative four-year deal in the 2014 offseason, Lowry was criticized for getting fat and lazy after that $48 million contract. People thought that he made it a point to stay out of shape since he was already getting paid with big dollars. But Lowry was always a winner. Knowing himself as such, Lowry's mindset coming into the new season was to prove all his critics and doubters wrong.

The first thing on Kyle Lowry's agenda was to improve his conditioning and get into the best shape possible. Since his high school playing years, Lowry had always been stubby. For a guy barely standing 6 feet tall, he was very thick and was robust enough to bully taller guys when trying to get to the basket. A lot of Lowry's game was predicated on his size and strength. However, being thick and chunky also meant that he was slower than he should have been and that he was not the best-conditioned player at his position.

Because of his subpar conditioning and his out-of-shape physique, Lowry decided to undergo a body transformation in the short offseason before the 2015-16 82-game stretch. He first sought the services of Joe Abunassar, the founder of Impact Basketball. Abunassar said that Lowry came to him wanting to play better and lose weight.[viii]

Joe Abunassar stated that Kyle Lowry's case was a lot different than what you see on reality TV. Lowry was never fat, according to him. The point guard was merely thick and chunky because that body type helped him in his style of play.[viii] But what he tried to do with Kyle Lowry was to get him in shape while keeping as much of his strength and muscle as possible for him to retain the same pit bull style he played on the court.

The trainer had his All-Star client in a strict training regimen and on a disciplined diet menu. At the earliest time possible during the day, Lowry would go on intense interval sprints uphill to burn as much fat as possible. But that was merely the beginning of his daily routine. After that, Lowry would go to the basketball court twice during the day to work on his game and keep his body working to shed those pounds. But he did not work out on the hard court individually. He was playing real and physical basketball with other professional players. That kept him in peak basketball shape and helped him retain the same playing style that got him his first All-Star bid in 2015.

After the intense running in the morning and after getting his shots in on the basketball court, Kyle Lowry would finish his daily routine lifting heavy in the weight room or doing extreme Pilates. What would usually tire out the average athlete was that Lowry did not have rest days. The only daily rest he was getting were 30-minute sweating sessions or when he would take a break for his meals.[viii]

On the subject of meals, Kyle Lowry's diet was something that would turn off any other human being. He was made to strictly and exclusively eat clean meals that usually involved egg whites and lean meat like fish or chicken as his protein sources. For the other nutritional and healthy needs, Lowry would snack on salads and a lot of kale. Sweets, desserts, other sugar sources, and fatty treats were strictly off the menu for Kyle Lowry.[viii]

Because of the strict workout and diet regimen he went through during the offseason, Kyle Lowry slimmed down from nearly 210 pounds to a little over 190. But Lowry did not look skinny at the end of it all. He looked lean with muscles that you could never see from his old body. Lowry had retained some of his strength and muscle mass while pushing himself to lose the fat that slowed him down in the 2014-15 season.

While younger All-Star NBA players would work on improving their shooting and dribbling skills on top of expanding their offensive arsenals, Kyle Lowry did something much more challenging. Even Dwane Casey confirmed that Lowry was the only player on his roster that could undergo such a routine.[ix] This was not an aging Kobe Bryant working out with Hakeem

Olajuwon for post moves. This was not Dirk Nowitzki perfecting his trademark fadeaway jumper. And this was not a prime Stephen Curry going through high-tech flashing light drills to improve his dribbling skills. This was a 29-year old All-Star putting himself on the strictest workout and diet program to improve his body and his conditioning at an age when most players would rather work on their skills and fundamentals.

After the body transformation that Lowry went through in the offseason, he had the whole world abuzz with a photo posted on a social media website. In that picture, Lowry's physique was on full display. He was no longer that chubby and stubby point guard. Instead, he looked so lean that his cuts and muscles were bulging out of his arms. Kyle Lowry, in a short span of time, was a different man and a different player as far as physique was concerned.

When the photo of Kyle Lowry came out, even his teammates were in shock with their star point guard's physical transformation. Patterson would immediately contact Lowry to confirm if his lean body was genuine and not a product of photo editing. The point guard would verify it. When the Raptors forward saw Lowry for the first time in person since the transformation, Patterson would recall how the point guard was always short and chunky since time immemorial. He was in such disbelief that he would even joke that the leaner Kyle Lowry was merely an evil twin brother.[ix]

Even Kyle Lowry's backcourt mate DeMar DeRozan could not believe the leaner and thinner physique that his running mate was sporting. He would immediately call up Lowry and tell him to come to Los Angeles, where DeRozan was residing, as soon as he could. DeRozan only wanted to see the transformation that his point guard had gone through. He would go on to say that he could never recall another NBA player in league history to have gone through such a major transformation in such a short span of time.

Despite knowing and playing with Lowry for more than three seasons already, DeMar DeRozan was not sure of what the transformation was going to do for their backcourt partnership. He did not know why Kyle Lowry wanted to lose weight. DeRozan knew that Lowry's style of play was always predicated on his chunky and strong body. He did not know what a leaner and slimmer Kyle Lowry could bring to the table.

But Kyle Lowry would prove to his teammates that he was still the same player. He told DeRozan that he could carry his teammates. He also said that the shape he was in would not hinder his style of play. Lowry merely got into that shape because it was a personal mission that he had to go through to improve his mindset and change his view of himself. The once stubby point guard now had abs to boast about and was expected to be better conditioned coming into the new season.

Head coach Dwane Casey was proud of what his point guard underwent. Aside from commending him for the effort that none of his other teammates would have been able to exert, he also said that Lowry's peak conditioning would prevent the point guard from going through the slump he faced after the All-Star break. It would also spare Lowry from going through another tough season of being the Raptors' scapegoat concerning criticisms.[ix]

Ever the self-aware player, Kyle Lowry always knew that he was the person blamed and criticized for the meltdown that his team faced in the second half of the 2014-15 NBA season. But that was not the reason he changed himself. He just wanted to become better physically and mentally. The 29-year-old point guard wanted people to be in awe of him again just like when he first started playing at the level of an All-Star.[ix] He would do just that in the 2015-16 season.

Early in the new season, Kyle Lowry immediately showed that he was in the best possible game shape of his entire decade-long

NBA career. He scored 23 points in his first game of the season while also leading the Raptors to five straight wins. In the middle of November, Lowry also scored at least 20 points in six straight outings while continuing to play a high level of basketball in all facets of the game.

On December 5, 2015, Kyle Lowry appeared unstoppable in a loss against the historic Golden State Warriors team. Playing against the MVP and leading scorer of the league did not scare the competitive Kyle Lowry. He would play Stephen Curry toe-to-toe throughout that bout. Though it came at a loss, Lowry had 41 points, seven assists, and four steals in that career night. He hit 14 of his 26 shots from the floor and 6 of his ten attempts from the three-point line. In the very next game, Lowry's shooting did not slow down when he made five three-pointers in a win against the Lakers. The player that was used to getting criticized for his lack of a jump shot was now one of the deadliest marksmen in the NBA.

After putting up that performance against the league-leading Warriors, Lowry and his team were as confident as they could have ever been. Throughout the regular season, the team was consistently the second seed in a surprisingly tougher Eastern Conference setup. They were even competing with the powerhouse Cleveland Cavaliers team and were constantly only a few games behind in wins. A much-improved Kyle Lowry was the catalyst of all that.

Early in January 2016, Kyle Lowry and the Raptors did not seem like they were slowing down. The team would win 11 straight games in that month and were 12-2 in January. In one of those games, the now-deadly outside shooter Kyle Lowry hit a career-high seven three-pointers in against the Brooklyn Nets. It was indeed becoming a common belief that the Toronto Raptors could only go as far as their point guard could take them. Lowry was rising with the Raptors.

Because of his consistent play in leading the Toronto Raptors to what was to become the best season in franchise history, Lowry was once again voted into the starting squad of the Eastern Conference All-Stars. At that point, there was almost no argument about Kyle Lowry's standings as a player. He was the best all-around point guard in the East because of his ability to put up an All-Star effort in all aspects of basketball.

Shortly after the All-Star break, Kyle Lowry recorded his first and only triple-double of the season in a win over the New York Knicks. He had 22 points, 11 rebounds, and 11 assists in that game. Two games after that performance, he posted a new career high for the second time that season. He had 43 points in a win against no less than the Cavs on February 26.

As the second half of the season unfolded, critics and analysts began to realize that there was no way that the Toronto Raptors were going to melt down the same way they did in the 2014-15 season. A part of the reason for that was Kyle Lowry, who never seemed like he was going to slow down and fall apart like he did just a year prior. The new-found conditioning and body transformation not only helped Lowry stay in shape the whole season, it also elevated his game to a level it had never gone to before. Kyle Lowry and the Toronto Raptors would never look back.

In what was his finest season yet, Kyle Lowry fully elevated his game and productivity. He averaged 21.2 points, which was three more points than what he averaged a year before. What was impressive about Lowry's scoring performance that year was his consistency. He never scored under 11 points in a season where he was always scoring in double digits. Kyle Lowry was also averaging 4.7 rebounds, 6.4 assists, and a career best 2.1 steals. Lowry also made a career-best 2.8 three-pointers per game while shooting 39% from that distance. He made a total of 212 three-pointers that season. Lowry was named to the All-NBA Third Team that year.

The consistent and improved play coming from Kyle Lowry had him being named among the league's top players that season and was even a contender for the MVP award. Lowry was sixth in win shares and real plus-minus among players that season. That simply shows how valuable of a leader and player Kyle Lowry was. Because of their leader's steady play throughout the season, the Raptors won at least 50 games for the first time in franchise history. Their 56-26 win-loss record was their franchise best. And, for the first time in team history as well, they were the second seed in the Eastern Conference and were only a game behind Cleveland.

Even Kyle Lowry himself was proud of what he had achieved. He believed that he was at the peak of his productivity and conditioning as a player and planned to stay that way even as he aged into his 30's. Lowry, at that point, still wanted to be a better player because he was a winner and wanted to stay competitive. He did not want to be a player that played in his late 30's just because he wanted to. Lowry still wanted to be able to contribute at a high level when he got to an advanced age in the NBA.[x]

Lowry and the rest of the league credit the point guard's transformation for the success that he and his team had during the regular season. Kyle Lowry just did not want to fold the way that he and his team had in the past season. He was on his way to prove that he did not want to make excuses and that he did not want critics to use his weight as a scapegoat for the Raptors' problems. The result of that was a historic season for him and his team. But, the real goal was still to win a championship. Kyle Lowry would never stray away from the target as the Raptors entered the 2016 playoffs.

The Toronto Raptors would be thoroughly tested in their quest to solidify their claim as one of the top teams in the Eastern Conference. Every series and every opponent they faced would push them to their limit. But the positive narrative one could get from their playoff run in 2016 was that they were already battle-tested and were going to be a tougher team in future seasons. Moreover, their leader Kyle Lowry was a changed player in that run.

Lowry and his second-seeded Raptors would face the Indiana Pacers in the first round. While typically the favorites in such a series, the Pacers defense would clamp down on the Raptors' stars. Lowry was limited to 11 points on 3 out of 13 shooting from the field when Indiana shockingly took Game 1 away from Toronto. Fortunately, the Raptors took charge in Game 2 and tied the series 1-1. Despite the win, it was obvious that Kyle

Lowry was struggling against the Pacer defense. He scored 18 points in that win but was only 4 out of 13 from the floor.

Lowry, who had struggled shooting in the last two games, would perform better in Game 3 when the Raptors took back the home court advantage from the Indiana Pacers. The star point guard scored 21 points and dished out eight assists. But, in the next game, the Indiana Pacers would once again put the clamps on Kyle Lowry, who would only go for 4 out of 12 shooting in that Game 4 loss.

Though Kyle Lowry would shoot only 27.3% from the field in Game 5, he was fortunate enough that his backcourt mate DeMar DeRozan matched Indiana star Paul George's output in that come-from-behind win. It would take a stellar defensive fourth quarter from the Raptors to pull closer to their opponents and take the win. Lowry, though still struggling from the field, managed to defend his opposing guards well. Nevertheless, the Indiana Pacers would blow out the Toronto Raptors in Game 6 to set up a do-or-die Game 7 in Canada.

Even though his postseason run was on the line, Kyle Lowry still could not get over the hump in what was an all-important seventh game in their first-round series against the Indiana Pacers. The All-Star point guard was still shooting blanks from the field while allowing Pacer guards George Hill and Monta Ellis to score well for Indiana. Lowry, who only scored 11 points in that game, had a lot of help from his bench players as the Toronto Raptors narrowly escaped the first round by winning a close one at home.

That win in Game 7 would take Kyle Lowry back to the second round for the first time since he helped the Houston Rockets push the Los Angeles Lakers to seven games back in 2009. Though Lowry was delighted to have driven his Raptors to a second-round appearance for the first time since joining the team, he had an ugly series against the Pacers. He never shot above 40% against the Indiana defense while struggling to contain the backcourt of the Pacers. If the Raptors would even dream of getting deeper in the playoffs, Lowry had to perform better.

Kyle Lowry knew that he had to get over his shooting slump somehow for his team to beat the Miami Heat in the second round of the 2016 postseason. Unfortunately, the slump continued when he was limited to his worst playoff performance that season. In Game 1 of that series, Kyle Lowry would only shoot 23% from the floor and was limited to only 7 points. It was the first time that season that Lowry was limited to single-digit scoring. It came at the worst of times as the Miami Heat took that bout from them.

Similar to how they bounced back versus the Indiana Pacers after dropping Game 1, the Toronto Raptors would tie the series 1-1 in Game 2. Though he was still practically shooting blanks from the floor, Kyle Lowry did not shy away from taking shots after shots on his way to 18 points. The effort from the point guard was just enough to give his team a four-point cushion at the end of 48 minutes.

After nine games of practically being invisible in the Toronto Raptors' challenging playoff run, Kyle Lowry would finally explode for one of his best postseason performances yet in Game 3. He would almost singlehandedly take back home court advantage for his team by scoring 33 points on a positive shooting clip from the field. He hit 5 of his eight three-pointers while going for 58% from the floor in that win.

But, just as quick as Lowry caught fire in Game 3, he would have his worst shooting clip in the 2016 playoffs in Game 4 when the Miami Heat beat them to tie the series 2-2. Kyle Lowry was merely 2 out of 11 from the field though he played all other facets of the game well. But what the Raptors needed from him was his scoring because none of the other starters were contributing. In fact, backup point guard Cory Joseph played better than Lowry in that loss.

While Lowry's focus was to win and that he would not mind his backup playing better than him, there was no way that a bench player was going to outshine him again. In one of the few instances that both Kyle Lowry and DeMar DeRozan played well, the point guard had 25 points, ten rebounds, six assists, and three steals to lead the way for the Raptors, who were up 3-2 after that win. Unfortunately for them, Miami would force Game 7 by winning the next game by 12 points.

Facing a chance to proceed to the second round, Kyle Lowry would make sure he was not going to be an afterthought or background player just as he was when they beat the Pacers in seven games. He was going to make an impact as the Toronto Raptors' leader. Interestingly enough, Game 6 turned out to be a battle of point guards that both used to be teammates back in the Houston Rockets. It was Kyle Lowry versus Goran Dragic.

Flashback to the 2011-12 season, Kyle Lowry and Goran Dragic were the top point guards in Houston. After former starter Aaron Brooks had been traded a season back, Lowry usurped him as the starter coming into the 2011-12 season. He would play well for the Rockets despite not being uncomfortable with

McHale's system. Unfortunately, he faced an injury in the middle of the season and was sidelined because of it.

When Lowry was recuperating from his injury, Goran Dragic took the starting point guard spot and electrified the Houston Rockets' fans with his fast-paced style of play and ability to score and put up points in a hurry. Dragic earned the adoration of the fans and coaches as well. His emergence suddenly made Lowry dispensable, even as the latter returned to full health. Lowry, who was relegated to doing bench duties at the final part of the season, was traded to the Raptors during the offseason of 2012. As we know, Lowry emerged as the Raptors' best player while Dragic did not do badly himself in his stints after Houston.

Going back to Game 6 of the Toronto Raptors' second-round series against the Miami Heat, both Kyle Lowry and Goran Dragic were now running their teams and were trying to push through to the Eastern Conference Finals. The two point guards would try to outplay each other as they made shot after shot in that backcourt battle. But it was the All-Star that emerged the winner in the personal battle, but not in the war. Kyle Lowry, who had 36 points, beat out Dragic's 30 markers. However, it was Dragic who was able to force a Game 7 because of his performance.

Coming into Game 7, revenge and victory were the narratives going through Kyle Lowry's mentality when he would finally try to dispatch his opponents in an intensely-fought seven-game series. As an encore to his 36-point performance in Game 6, Lowry delivered 35 markers in Game 7. Other than that, he was all over the floor. The All-Star point guard also had seven rebounds, nine assists, and four steals while thoroughly outplaying Dragic, who finished with only 16 points. This time, Lowry won both the personal battle and the war because he was on his way to the Conference Finals for the first time in his career and franchise history.

The second round victory over the Miami Heat catapulted the Toronto Raptors into the deepest playoff run the franchise has ever gotten. Formerly one of the feeder teams in the NBA in the sense that their purpose was to allow other teams to win games and get deeper into the postseason, the Raptors were now legitimate title contenders.

Though it was arguably the best Toronto Raptors team ever assembled in NBA history, the man responsible for taking them that far was their point guard Kyle Lowry. Vince Carter, for all his superstar qualities and out-of-this-world athleticism, could not take them that far. Chris Bosh, who was one of the best power forwards of the era and who was always in the All-Star

105

mix, could not take the Raptors that far. None of Toronto Raptors' franchise superstars took them to greater heights before a small and competitive point guard did.

It was Kyle Lowry, in all of his 6-foot frame, who led the Toronto Raptors to the Eastern Conference Finals for the first time in the team's history. This was a player that never became a starter until his fifth season in the NBA. This was a point guard that could not become an All-Star until his ninth year in the league. Lowry was an underdog that carried the load of a hopeful franchise on his small shoulders.

Kyle Lowry's and the Raptors' underdog status would become even more glaring than it ever had before when they faced the Cleveland Cavaliers in the Conference Finals. LeBron James, Kyrie Irving, and Kevin Love together in one team would scare any other franchise before the battle even started. It was no wonder they swept every opponent they faced in the playoffs to get to the East Finals. But Lowry was a competitor that never backed down from anybody. That quality would rub off on his team.

Despite having all the heart and competitive hunger in the world, the Toronto Raptors were not spared from their embarrassing losses in Cleveland. The Cavaliers utterly demolished the

106

Raptors in Game 1 of their East Finals series. In that 31-point embarrassment, Lowry could not even get off a shot, much less defend Irving on the other end. He finished with 8 points while allowing Kyrie to score 27.

Game 2 was not much different regarding outcome and effort on the part of the Raptors. While the bench came out to play and to cover the mistakes that the starters were committing, the Cavaliers' offensive and defensive strategies pushed the Raptors into a corner unable to defend or even muster up any offense. Moreover, it was also another weak output for Kyle Lowry after finishing the final two games against the Heat with terrific numbers.

Coming into Game 3 in Toronto, everyone already counted the Raptors out. The narratives were apparent. The Cavs were simply too hungry and strong on both ends for them to defeat. Nobody could stop or defend James. Irving was also scoring at will as well much to the dismay of Lowry, who was a terrific defender himself. It was expected that another four-game sweep was in the making for Cleveland, who were clearly the title favorites in the East.

Kyle Lowry has heard it all from the very beginning of his NBA career. He was uncoachable. He was too short. He could not start on a team, much less even lead them to the playoffs. He was not an All-Star talent. And he could not perform at his best in the playoffs. Those were all the criticisms he has faced in his decade-long NBA career. But, over the course of that decade, he had proven all doubters wrong. He had nothing more to prove even if he beat the Cavaliers. But Lowry was a winner. He did not want to beat Cleveland because he wanted to prove something. He just wanted to do it because he wanted to compete and win.

Coming into Game 3 as the clear underdogs and as the probable next victim of a Cavalier sweep, the Toronto Raptors suddenly looked like a very different team. While everybody in the world had them beat as early as their loss in Game 2, the team never doubted themselves, especially with a competitive and ferocious Kyle Lowry leading the charge. In Game 3, the world saw a whole new species of Raptors.

Toronto matched and even outplayed Cleveland's efforts in Game 3. Center Bismack Biyombo was out there to grab every miss that bounced off the rim despite his 6'9" height. DeMar DeRozan had been taking advantage of mismatches on the offensive end to score one of his best games. And Kyle Lowry was out there playing his pit bull style of basketball.

Kyle Lowry, who finished with 20 points on 54% shooting, was all over the floor in Game 3. He was making life easy for his teammates while also putting the clamps on Kyrie Irving, who top-scored in Games 1 and 2. And when he would get the chance to defend LeBron at the post in many of the Cavaliers' efforts to get their best player a favorable mismatch, Lowry would not back down from the much bigger opponent. Above all that, his competitive nature rubbed off on the bench, who contributed well to the Raptors' charge. The result of their efforts and hustle was a 15-point win the right to silence their doubters.

While the Cleveland Cavaliers put up a better effort in Game 4, the Toronto Raptors maintained the same energy and hunger that had got them within one game away from tying the series. In Game 4, the backcourt duo of Lowry and DeRozan was on full display. They were practically unguardable on their way to a combined scoring effort of 67 points. Those 67 points were the most that the two combined for in any game since teaming up back in 2012. The result of the partnership was another win for the Raptors and a series tie for the team that made the Cavaliers look mortal in the postseason.

While the series was still far from over, the two wins in Toronto were already moral victories for the Raptors that came in as obvious underdogs and as the "other team" among the four squads left in the playoffs. Nobody even gave them a chance against the Cleveland Cavaliers, who many thought would sweep them. But they came out with two wins after four games and proved their doubters wrong. They turned the series into a virtual three-game battle. This was no longer the squad that was used to choking in the first round. They were ready to win a title in one of the most opportune times in franchise history.

While the Toronto Raptors tried to fight the good fight, they were again not spared from an embarrassing loss to the Cavaliers when the series went back to Cleveland. Without the energy emanating from their faithful fans in Toronto, the Raptors had nothing but blanks left in their holster in Game 5. After combining for 67 points in Game 4, Lowry and DeRozan could not even score half of that in that 38-point Game 5 loss to the Cavs.

Facing elimination in Game 6, Kyle Lowry was in the mood for carrying the team all by his lonesome, similar to how he did when he arguably single-handedly defeated the Heat in Game 7 of their matchup. Lowry's shooting was at its finest in the playoffs as he refused to give up to the mightier Cavs. Unfortunately for him, he was merely one man against an army. Kyle Lowry's 35-point effort went unnoticed when the only other Raptor that scored in double digits was his backcourt mate. Meanwhile, Cleveland played like a team despite being in hostile territory as they defeated their opponents on the latter's own home floor.

That Game 6 loss to the Cleveland Cavaliers signified the end of the deepest playoff run that the Toronto Raptors ever mustered up in franchise history. While failing to beat the Cavs and reaching the Finals was a disappointment for the team, they had nothing to be ashamed of after putting up a historic franchise postseason run. If the 2016 playoffs indicated anything for the Raptors, it would be that they were going to be one of the most terrifying Eastern Conference teams for years to come. We might even see them playing in the Finals when the stars are aligned correctly.

For Kyle Lowry, the whole 2015-16 season run up to his efforts in leading the Toronto Raptors deep into the 2016 postseason was his coming out party in the NBA. He first proved that he was All-Star quality when he made the 2015 Eastern All-Star team. But, in the last season, Lowry showed that he belonged among the most elite players in the NBA after being named to the All-NBA Third Team. This was a player that was drafted 24th overall and could not become an All-Star until his ninth season. But after finding his home in Toronto, Lowry showed

111

his quality as one of the best players in the NBA. Ever the competitive player, Kyle Lowry's star is not expected to fall any sooner in the next NBA seasons.

Chapter 5: Kyle Lowry's Personal Life

Kyle Lowry's parents are Marie Hollaway and Lonnie Lowry, Sr. The two were separated during much of Kyle's childhood. Because of this, Kyle Lowry was raised by his mother Marie with the help of his grandmother. His mother had to work two jobs just to support her family's wants and needs. And without a father figure in the family, Kyle Lowry turned to his older brother Lonnie Jr. for the help and guidance that a dad would usually provide a family.

Kyle and Lonnie Jr. were as close as brothers can be. It was Lonnie who helped Kyle love the game of basketball by bringing the younger Lowry to different ballparks and local games in Philadelphia. Lonnie Jr. was indeed a good influence on his brother's future, especially because the senior Lonnie did not even bother to be present in both of his sons' lives despite living merely a few minutes away from the Lowry brothers.

While Kyle Lowry once hoped that his father would become more interested in his life, he ultimately gave up in that regard when Lonnie Sr. did not hold up his promise of spending a whole day with Kyle. The younger Lowry waited and waited that day, but his father never came. His father's absence was one of the reasons why Kyle grew up having troubles respecting male authority figures in basketball.

While Kyle Lowry would grow up having trust issues with his coaches, he grew to trust Dave Distel, one of his mentors in the many youth leagues he joined as a young basketball prodigy. Distel earned the trust of Lowry and was one of the father figures that the star point guard looked up to, even when he was already an NBA player, by remaining as a consistent figure in the young star's life.

Another basketball coach that Kyle Lowry grew to trust was Billy Lange, who was formerly with Villanova. When Villanova was actively pursuing the services of Lowry for college, it was Lange who tried to convince the point guard to join their college team. He would get to know Kyle Lowry on a personal level throughout the recruitment process, and he eventually earned the point guard's trust. Lange was one of the reasons Lowry chose to go to Villanova.

Billy Lange would eventually accept a job at Navy just as Lowry was about to go to Villanova. Kyle Lowry, upset about the decision, would stay out of touch with Lange. It was only in 2011 when Lowry was officially the Houston Rockets' starter that the two reunited and resumed communication. But it was not without Lowry expressing his disappointment towards Lange's decision of leaving him several years back.

In 2013, Kyle Lowry would marry Ayahna Cornish, his longtime girlfriend. The two met back when they were in high school attending Cardinal Dougherty. Back then, Kyle was not the only high school star in the school. Ayahna herself was great basketball talent and averaged 18.7 points, nine rebounds, and seven assists in her senior year in high school. Her 1,782 points were a school record.[xi]

While Kyle was playing for Villanova, Ayahna was over at St. Joseph starring in their women's basketball team. Ayahna brought her stellar talent over to the school and was St. Joseph's best player in her sophomore and junior years. But her basketball career in St. Joseph's was derailed by an ACL injury in her junior season.[xi]

In 2011, Ayahna would bear Kyle their first son. Karter was one of the reasons for Kyle Lowry's quick maturity. At 24, Kyle had no idea how to be a father, especially because he never experienced having one in the first place. Neither he nor Ayahna knew what they were doing with Karter. It was the couple's mutual trust that helped them get through that tough time especially when Kyle was still trying to make his name in the NBA.[xii]

Coincidentally, it was during the start of Kyle Lowry's fatherhood that he first became a starter in his NBA career. He said that the difficult stage of getting through fatherhood tested him to his limits and matured him faster than he would have thought. It helped him change as a person and challenged him mentally.[xii] Just a season later, he almost became an All-Star as the best point guard of the Rockets.

Kyle Lowry's fatherhood problems with Karter also got him to realize how difficult it was for his past coaches to mentor him whenever he was acting like his stubborn, hardheaded self. As the narratives go, Lowry was uncoachable early in his career because he found it difficult to trust coaches. But his episodes with his son made him realize how difficult it was for his coaches to handle him.[xii]

Lowry always found it a challenge to make Karter eat food ideal for toddlers. It would frustrate him whenever his son would not do what he told him to do. That was when Kyle realized that he was in the same position as Kevin McHale was when they were still both in Houston. McHale would make Lowry do things that he thought were going to make the point guard and the team

116

better. But Kyle never understood that until he experienced being a father.[xii]

The difficulties of being a father turned out to make Kyle Lowry better as a person and player. Not long after he was still changing Karter's diapers, Lowry would become the undisputed leader of the Toronto Raptors. Later on, he would become a two-time All-Star mature enough to take his team to heights it had never seen before. Understanding how tough it was to become a coach and father figure to a younger person, Lowry would form a good bond with head coach Dwane Casey, who would also learn to trust the keys to the team in the hands of his star point guard.

Aside from gleaming with joy whenever he talks about his family and having good relationships with his coaches in high school and college, Kyle Lowry also has a good rapport with his Raptors GM Masai Ujiri and his mentor Chauncey Billups.

Having heard about Lowry's perceived attitude problems when he first came to Toronto, Ujiri talked some sense into his point guard to try to change his outlook on his team. On the other hand, Billups, who was also as fiery and tenacious as Lowry was, told the younger point guard that maturity was the key to making himself a better leader for the Raptors.[xii] Lowry's trust in those veterans would help him become the elite star that he is today.

Chapter 6: Kyle Lowry's Legacy and Future

When you look at the annals of NBA history and all the players that have gone through the league, you might never see a player that endured and braved through nine whole seasons as a professional just to get to call himself an All-Star. All in all, it took Kyle Lowry an entire decade in the NBA to even see his name being mentioned among the league's most elite players.

While a similar player like Chauncey Billups experienced the same nine-year journey to stardom that Lowry went through, none of them had passed through the early years of getting doubted and criticized that the Raptors' star point guard had to endure in his 10-year NBA career.

Unlike most of his peers, Kyle Lowry was not even one of the most sought-after names in his draft class. He was only chosen 24th in the 2006 NBA Draft. While getting selected in the first round is already an accomplishment in itself, it was not what a winner and competitor like Kyle Lowry had hoped for. Early in his career, he had to battle for minutes against battle-tested veterans and more favored young point guards. He also had to endure injuries and criticisms about his attitude. Because of those factors, Kyle Lowry often found himself on the bench as merely a backup to the experienced and favored playmakers.

Despite finally getting a break as a starter in the middle of his 20's, Kyle Lowry's reputation concerning his ability to take criticism and instructions from authority figures such as his coaches. His inability to see eye-to-eye with most of his coaches often had him clashing with them regarding ideologies and beliefs of what a point guard is and how the position should be played.

However, it was only when he finally understood what it meant to be a leader and finally matured as a person and player that he saw the error of his ways. Lowry began to form bonds with his teammates, and he even learned how to trust his coaches. Trust was always the deciding factor and the word that best described his journey in the NBA. By trusting everyone that mattered to the team and his personal development, Kyle Lowry exploded into the scenes as a changed man.

The mental change that Lowry went through helped him become the All-Star he is right now, and it also helped him get the Toronto Raptors to its best season yet as a franchise. He earned the adoration of his teammates, his coaches, his franchise, and his city's country as well. Kyle Lowry's star reached an all-time high that no other Raptor franchise player has gone before. All it took was for him to have the right mentality and the proper outlook towards becoming a leader.

What Kyle Lowry's NBA journey to stardom means for the league is that it represents all the other professional players that have struggled to get a break in their career. Kyle Lowry depicted the late first round and second round picks that were not given a chance to shine. He represented those undrafted and still wanting to find a spot in the league. He represented the misunderstood who never had the opportunity to mature because they were written off so quickly. Kyle Lowry gave hope to players that still work so hard to get a chance to showcase their talents.

While not everyone might get the chance to develop into the elite player that Lowry is today, it does not mean that they will never find their respective place in the NBA because belonging in the league means more than just becoming a superstar and leader of a franchise. It means having a team to call home and having your coaches and your teammates trust you. That was what Kyle Lowry valued the most aside from winning.

Kyle Lowry's journey is not only about how he could influence people struggling to find a spot in the NBA. It could also help the average Joe, who is barely making ends meet. What Lowry showed us was that the right mentality and the right attitude towards work and towards grasping the leadership mantle will more than likely change the way you perceive your personal endeavors. A change in perception and attitude towards our endeavors will more than likely yield the same positive results that Kyle Lowry saw.

As Kyle Lowry, who is now entering the second decade of his NBA career, continues his quest to reach the pinnacle of professional success in the league, one might wonder how long he could sustain playing at an elite level. He only attained it at a time when most other players in the league were slowly declining past their prime.

But one only has to remember how hard Kyle Lowry fought on his way to superstardom. One only has to remember how ferocious and competitive he always was when trying to win. When one remembers those, one can be rest assured knowing that Kyle Lowry would always put his full effort into staying hungry, competitive, and focused. One can rest assured knowing that Kyle Lowry's journey is far from over.

Final Word/About the Author

I was born and raised in Norwalk, Connecticut. Growing up, I could often be found spending many nights watching basketball, soccer, and football matches with my father in the family living room. I love sports and everything that sports can embody. I believe that sports are one of most genuine forms of competition, heart, and determination. I write my works to learn more about influential athletes in the hopes that from my writing, you the reader can walk away inspired to put in an equal if not greater amount of hard work and perseverance to pursue your goals. If you enjoyed *Kyle Lowry: The Inspiring Story of One of Basketball's All-Star Guards,* please leave a review! Also, you can read more of my works on *Calvin Johnson, Colin Kaepernick, Aaron Rodgers, Peyton Manning, Tom Brady, Russell Wilson, Michael Jordan, LeBron James, Kyrie Irving, Klay Thompson, Stephen Curry, Kevin Durant, Russell Westbrook, Anthony Davis, Chris Paul, Blake Griffin, Kobe Bryant, Joakim Noah, Scottie Pippen, Carmelo Anthony, Kevin Love, Grant Hill, Tracy McGrady, Vince Carter, Patrick Ewing, Karl Malone, Tony Parker, Allen Iverson, Hakeem Olajuwon, Reggie Miller, Michael Carter-Williams, John Wall, James Harden, Tim Duncan, Steve Nash, Pau Gasol, Marc Gasol, Jimmy Butler, Dirk Nowitzki, Draymond Green, Pete Maravich,*

Kawhi Leonard, Dwyane Wade, Ray Allen, Paul George, Paul Pierce, Manu Ginobili, and Larry Bird in the Kindle Store. If you love basketball, check out my website at claytongeoffreys.com to join my exclusive list where I let you know about my latest books and give you lots of goodies.

Like what you read? Please leave a review!

I write because I love sharing the stories of influential people like Kyle Lowry with fantastic readers like you. My readers inspire me to write more so please do not hesitate to let me know what you thought by leaving a review! If you love books on life, basketball, or productivity, check out my website at claytongeoffreys.com to join my exclusive list where I let you know about my latest books. Aside from being the first to hear about my latest releases, you can also download a free copy of *33 Life Lessons: Success Principles, Career Advice & Habits of Successful People*. See you there!

Clayton

References

[i] Zarum, Dave. "Leap of Faith." *Sports Net.* Web

[ii] Rashidi, Kevin. "Q&A With Marie Hollaway, Mother of Kyle Lowry: On Her Son and the City of Toronto." *SB Nation.* 21 May 2016. Web

[iii] Abrams, Jonathan. "You Can Count on Me". *Grant Land.* 23 September 2014. Web

[iv] "Kyle Lowry NBA Draft Scouting Report". *Draft Express.* 30 April 2006. Web

[v] Thomsen, Ian. "All-Star Starting Nod Just the Beginning for Raptors' Lowry". *NBA.com.* 7 February 2015. Web

[vi] Windhorst, Brian. "Injuries Taking Heavy Toll on Raptors' Lowry." *ESPN.* 22 April 2015. Web

[vii] Ewing, Lori. "Kyle Lowry's Health Questioned Amid Raptors' Playoff Struggles". *The Canadian Press.* 23 April 2015. Web

[viii] Rutherford, Kristina. "Kyle Lowry's Trainer Breaks Down Off-Season Transformation". *Sportsnet.* 28 October 2015. Web

[ix] Herbert, James. "Kyle Lowry's Shocking Weight Loss Could be Huge Gain for Raptors". *CBS Sports.* 28 September 2015. Web

[x] Mazzeo, Mike. "Kyle Lowry Lifted Up His Game by Dropping the Pounds". *ESPN.* 23 January 2016. Web

[xi] "Ayahna Cornish-Lowry, Kyle's Wife: 5 Fast Facts You Need to Know". *Heavy Sports.* 14 February 2016. Web

[xii] Johnston, Mike. "Kyle Lowry on How Fatherhood Changed Him". *The Players' Tribune.* 11 February 2016. Web

Made in the USA
Middletown, DE
30 October 2017